The Oil Economy of Kuwait

The Oil Economy of Kuwait

Dr Y. S. F. Al-Sabah

Kegan Paul International Ltd
London and Boston

First published in 1980
by Kegan Paul International Ltd
39 Store Street,
London WC1E 7DD and
9 Park Street,
Boston, Mass. 02108, USA
Set in Press Roman by
Hope Services
Abingdon, Oxon
and printed in Great Britain by
Redwood Burn Ltd
Trowbridge & Esher
© Y. S. F. Al-Sabah 1980

ISBN 0 7103 0003 4

Contents

In memory of my father

Preface

The idea behind the writing of this book is not new. However, the fact that it was actually written was the result of continuous encouragement and insistence of many friends, both in the academic and business communities of the Arab and western worlds. The research behind the writing of this book has covered a long period, often interrupted by personal assignments and commitments throughout the world. However, it was not conducted under the auspices of any organization, either foreign or domestic, and the author accepts responsibility for the views contained within.

Y. S. F. Al-Sabah

Introduction

Kuwait has little recorded ancient history. Recent excavation on Failaka Island, however, indicates Greek settlement around 600 BC and probably it was also a stopping point for the other old civilizations of Mesopotamia, whose influence spread to other parts of the Ancient World through their sea-going culture. Contemporary studies have shown that the Babylonians and the Sumerians crossed the Gulf and the Indian Ocean using their famous reed boats — perhaps if more excavation were carried out on Failaka and the other islands off Kuwait, traces of some of the old Mesopotamian civilizations would be discovered. Indeed, until recently, some of the Kuwaiti fishermen used small reed boats called warjiah, which they built themselves from reed imported from southern Iraq and in a way similar to the Sumerian ones. Also, the Kuwaitis used water jars and reed plates for their domestic purposes, and these again were similar to vessels used by the Sumerians. Nevertheless, none of the present characteristics of Kuwait and its people has any connection with the country's ancient history.

With the advent of Islam and the increasing influence of the Arabs beyond the Arabian Peninsula some parts of the northern territory of Kuwait, in particular Kathma, became the battleground of the Moslem Arabs and the Persians. The former won a decisive battle under their famous leader Khalid Ibn Al-Waleed. The effects of that victory were far reaching, bringing about the conversion of the Persians to Islam — the influence of which was felt as far east as China. It was this Islamic-Arabic culture that became the main feature of Kuwait and that was carried by the tribes migrating from the heart of the Arab Peninsula.

There is no richness or diversity in the geography of Kuwait — the predominant factors are the desert and the sea, which have formed and shaped human occupation and organization. The challenge of the

1

environment to the inhabitants of Kuwait was harsh and unrelenting. The hostility of the desert to all kinds of human adaptation made the building of a civilized permanent community an impossible task. The lack of running water was the main factor underlying the nomadic way of life. Scarcity of all kinds made tribal wars the rule rather than the exception. Those writers who romanticize life in the desert do not really know it and only those who have lived in it understand it.

Nevertheless, the geographical location of Kuwait made it an ideal outlet for much of the hinterland of the Arabian Peninsula and it became an important commercial centre for the desert caravans, carrying various goods from Kuwait to Europe through Aleppo and other ports. Similarly, the sea routes carried the Iraqi goods to East Africa and India and the latter sent their trade to the Gulf ports and in particular to Kuwait as a commercial centre and transit town.

It was Kuwait's geographical position in relation to the major trade routes that gave it such political significance in the eyes of the major powers. The British were aware of the importance of Kuwait's location and its relation to their trade route to India and the Far East. The Germans were even more conscious of this, and their only way to challenge Britain seemed to be to gain access to Kuwait and thus to India and the Far East. Consequently, they planned their railway system to Anathol in Turkey to be linked to Baghdad, Basra and Kuwait. The Russians, too, were interested in Kuwait and the Gulf region — once again for the access provided to India and the Far East. Among several railway plans made by the Russians was the project to connect Tripoli on the Eastern coast of the Mediterranean with Kuwait. At the same time, several Russian ships and missions visited Kuwait, the main purpose being to undermine the influence of Britain in Kuwait and the Gulf region as a whole and to replace the nominal power of Turkey in that part of the world.

Although British politicians and diplomats remained undecided about their position in Kuwait certain events indicating the active interest of other foreign powers accelerated a clarification of the British position. This began when Shaikh Mubarak Al-Sabah came to power in 1896. He wished to secure British protection against Ottoman threats and, although Britain remained initially reluctant to extend its full legal protection to him, by the year 1899 it had realized beyond doubt the importance of Kuwait and of Shaikh Mubarak Al-Sabah and a treaty of protection was signed.

Shaikh Mubarak understood power politics in its best terms and dealt with Turkey, France, Russia and Britain with a shrewdness and clarity of mind as to which power would be predominant in the Gulf region. Despite the internal and external turmoil engulfing Kuwait and the Arabian Peninsula, as a result of strife between the great powers and because of internal tribal wars, Shaikh Mubarak was able to determine the independent status of Kuwait. It should be said, however, that Britain was of great help to him and, after his death, when his successors were subject to tribal and religious invasions, all were repulsed by force. In fact, it was Shaikh Mubarak and Britain together who decided the present political status of Kuwait.

Shaikh Mubarak was actively involved with the well-being of the Kuwaitis. He encouraged trade and extended help and protection to the seafarers and pearl-diving boats. His successor, Shaikh Salem Mubarak Al-Sabah, put more emphasis on internal security than on foreign affairs and he appointed a member of his family — Shaikh Sabah Duaij Al-Sabah — as head of the internal security department. Shaikh Sabah Duaij Al-Sabah became famous for his hard work in laying the foundations of internal security and he was further successful in eradicating all kinds of theft throughout Kuwait.[1]

Such internal security, together with the importance of its geographical position, have brought prosperity to Kuwait and this has encouraged people from Persia, Iraq and other parts of the Arab Peninsula to settle in Kuwait. Such immigration has been increasing since the early years of the nineteenth century and has continued until the present time.

Part of this trend was through an increasing number of foreign merchants establishing themselves in Kuwait. This led to opposition from the old-established Kuwaiti business men. When Shaikh Ahmed Al-Jaber Al-Sabah, Shaikh Salem's successor, increased the customs duty on imports discontent was aggravated further among the Kuwaiti merchants. This was at a time when there was general discontent in Kuwait and people were demanding more say in the affairs of state.

Such demands were even further aggravated when the Kuwaiti authorities dissolved an elected educational council and replaced it with an appointed one. As a result other members of different elected councils resigned in protest against the government's action. These events brought about a division within the political movement in Kuwait. On the one hand there was a group wanting direct British rule, as in Aden, or an effective British adviser, as in Bahrain; on the other, there was a group wanting a ruling family but with its power limited by a parliamentary system.

It is perhaps unfortunate that at such a time of unrest in Kuwait relations between the Political Agent, Captain de Gaurry, and the ruler were less than cordial. De Gaurry felt that the time for one-man rule in Kuwait was passed but Shaikh Ahmad was naturally reluctant to relinquish his traditionally autocratic role as ruler. However, mounting pressure from the merchants and from various factions, for some measure of representative assembly, finally led to the election of the first Legislative Council in Kuwait on 2 July 1938.

The first Legislative Council did not last more than a few months. Nevertheless it achieved a lot. In the field of commerce all kinds of customs duties on imports were changed. On transit goods only half the official customs duty was paid; however, no customs duty was to be paid on goods carried on ships calling into Kuwait (never charged on other ships in a Kuwaiti port). All customs duties were to be paid in money rather than in kind, as had been the case before 1938. To fight smuggling, a special police force was formed to protect the sea coast of Kuwait, and for internal security the Legislative Council formed a new department of public security.

As far as education was concerned more Palestinian teachers were invited to Kuwait to help with both male and female education. It must be said at this point that the Palestinian educational system, which was based on the British system, served very well in Kuwait. As to foreign relations with Britain the only change during the period of the first Legislative Council was a certain strengthening. It was in Britain's interest to see a kind of national consensus towards its dealings with Shaikh Mubarak and his successors. However, above all its other accomplishments the Legislative Council initiated a national budget to be separate from that of the ruler and to be managed under the authority of the Legislative Council.

With the exception of the events leading to the dissolution of the first Legislative Council, Kuwait continued its economic and social development gradually and without serious interruption, until the Second World War. After the war economic development continued but this time with unprecedented growth due to the development of the oil industry. It was the period after the Second World War that transformed the economy of Kuwait from a dependence on seafaring to a complete reliance on the export of crude oil.

The development of the oil industry led to increasing changes in

Kuwait. There was a huge influx of foreigners due to the higher wage gravity. Government expenditure was increasing on all fronts, resulting in a welfare state where inhabitants paid no tax of any kind. The people did not bear the cost of their development. Commerce flourished based on the import of all kinds of goods — sold in the Kuwaiti market at very high profit margins. Banks and investment companies gradually began to develop as a kind of permanent economic institution. Kuwait's involvement in foreign affairs became more complex through its relations with the members of the Arab League and other nations. Its important role as a donor of aid expedited its reputation in world affairs. Its ambitious businessmen widened their area of investment to include the rest of the world. Government capital surplus was deposited with almost every major international bank, and investments ranged from short-term deposits to real-estate businesses. Its main concern became how to protect its oil wealth and its financial resources abroad. Decreasing oil production and increasing oil prices secured the former; with regard to the latter, however, Kuwait's financial resources remain, and will always remain, exposed to world inflation and currency fluctuations.

Kuwait was similar to any other Arab country looking forward to its political and economic independence. The social movement of the 1930s continued and gained more strength by having new blood in its political stream in the 1950s. There were strikes and effective political demands for a democratic system. One should not ignore the role of the later ruler, Shaikh Abdula Al-Salem Al-Sabah, who was effective in establishing the first Legislative Council in 1938. He was even more effective in responding to and sympathizing with the political demands of the leaders of the socio-political movement in Kuwait. Britain was also aware of the main political groupings in Kuwait and saw no harm in their participation in a political democratic system. Accordingly, Kuwait's treaty with Britain of 1899 was replaced by another treaty of friendship on 19 June 1961, by which Kuwait gained its full political independence from Britain. No sooner was this achieved than General Kassem of Iraq started his political claim to Kuwait. Britain was called upon in a military capacity and the matter was resolved. However, those political claims were accelerating the establishment of a political-democratic system in Kuwait.

A year after independence, a constituent assembly was established in Kuwait to draw up a constitution for its parliament. During the sessions of the constitutional assembly many diverse political views were expressed as to the type of political system that Kuwait should adopt. One group wanted a theological state, another wanted a completely secular state; a third group wanted a mixture of the first and second. On the other hand, very little discussion covered the status of political parties and interest groups. The various groups and factions were eliminated, in theory, by constitution but established themselves later on in the parliament as *de facto* political institutions, whether they called themselves parties or were known by other names.

A Kuwaiti parliament was established in 1963 and was lively and beneficial during its life. It increased the level of administrative efficiency, and it brought a more rational approach to budgeting and state expenditure, though it did not control them. It asked for effective economic planning, though it did not manage to impose it on the government as a means of an economic way of life. The problem was that the political opposition of the young parliament was fighting on several fronts. They were trying to convince some of the other members, who had come to parliament on ethnic, religious and tribal grounds, of their own ideas and programmes. (They realized in the end, however, that there was no point in doing so, except to expose them to the Kuwaitis.) They were fighting the oil companies. They were introducing new legislation for the advancement of Kuwait. They were earning Kuwait its correct place in foreign affairs. In other words, they were trying to accomplish a great deal within a very short time – which they did. The Kuwaiti parliament and its free press were the envy of the rest of the Arab world.

It is interesting to note that in the 1930s the upper merchant class was the driving force behind the establishment of the first Legislative Council in Kuwait. At that time the government depended on the levy of taxes, which was supplied by the activities of the merchants. They were constantly raising the issue of no taxation without representation. In the 1960s, however, instead of paying taxes the merchants were accumulating substantial wealth based on government expenditure. They became dependent on the economic role of the government. However, they were aspiring, through the parliament, to political power in addition to their economic wealth through the government's constant huge expenditure. When the merchants realized the effective role of the parliament, they were the first to be happy at its dissolution on 16 August 1976: some of the legislation of the Kuwaiti parliament was dangerously close to impinging on their own interests, such as prices, control of banking and investment companies, and the regulation of an unruly stock exchange and of speculation. In other words, the upper merchant class was unhappy about the rising political power of some of the national political movements in the parliament. They were afraid not of their competition but of their power of control.

The role of the ethnic and tribal members in the parliament created divisions and political groupings based on ethnic and tribal ambitions within Kuwaiti society. Tribal organization obviously does not fit the criteria for a modern state system and their presence caused great difficulties. Their constant clash with the national members of parliament infuriated those Kuwaitis who refused to accept ethnicism and tribalism as bases of national development and progress. It was these clashes, and nothing else, that led to the dissolution of the Kuwaiti parliament. Several writers have ascribed the dissolution to foreign powers, but this is not the case. It was a Kuwaiti problem and was dealt with by Kuwaitis without any external influence. (Recent regional political development, however, might well accelerate the re-establishment of a parliament in Kuwait.)

The absence of a parliament has created a political vacuum — it was a symbol of the collective will in Kuwait. For any political action taken by Kuwait against any political incident inside or outside Kuwait, there was no one individual to blame, only the parliament, which represented the Kuwaitis. If the government wished to restrict the entry of more foreign labour it could do so through parliament. If it wanted to take any undesirable decision regarding its relations with any of the other Arab states, it could implement these decisions through parliament. In other words there was a collective vehicle making the decisions and assuming consequent responsibility, rather than particular individuals in the government. In the absence of a parliament, any decision taken by the government becomes the responsibility of executive members of the ruling family.

The re-establishment of the Kuwaiti parliament should be considered not merely desirable but necessary. Its necessity arises from the political vacuum we have already noted and from the fulfilment of a human desire for political representation and equality. However, in making its appointments the government should take full account of the experiences of the previous parliament and of the requirements necessary for a modern parliamentary system. Experience has shown the drawbacks of appointments made on ethnic and tribal bases. A minimum standard of education should be made obligatory for prospective members, and the distribution and demarcation of electoral constituencies should be changed in such a way as to reduce the effects of tribalism and ethnicism during the election.

The future role of the parliament should be qualitative rather than quantitative. It should concentrate on the improvement of the quality of life in Kuwait. It should improve the efficiency of government management. It should aim to reduce, but could probably not eliminate, economic waste in all spheres of Kuwaiti society — economic waste became synonymous with prosperity and lavishness on a large scale. It should aim to create better equal opportunities for all Kuwaitis, with great emphasis upon the individual rather than upon his or her family. The past parliament concentrated on the emancipation of the oil industry from foreign exploitation; a new parliament should concentrate on the freedom of the oil industry from bureaucracy. A new parliament should devote more time to the discussion of Kuwait's foreign investment, including the Kuwait Fund for Arab Economic Development. These objectives should command greater parliamentary attention and improvement will, hopefully, be achieved. The state enterprises should be reviewed in parliament and their management subjected to a critical examination. Government services of all kinds should be widely discussed in any future parliament, with the hope that their level of efficiency will thus be improved. Equality of income should be the subject-matter of discussion both inside and outside any future parliament.

Problems facing Kuwait

The title of this book reflects the nature of the problem in Kuwait: the export-orientated oil industry is the only economic base for the whole economy. Figure 1 shows more clearly how the economic system works through financial inflows and outflows.

The oil sector in Kuwait is very profitable due to world demand. The oil companies, apart from their small local-factor payments, pay directly to the government a huge amount of foreign exchange through taxes and royalties. Now that almost all the oil industry in Kuwait is government owned almost all the proceeds from oil exports accrue to the government.

Oil revenue accounts for 97 per cent of the government's income.

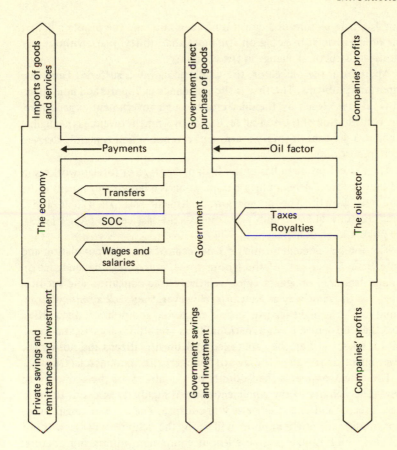

Figure 1

Some of this oil revenue is poured into the economy through capital expenditure on social overheads, current expenditure, capital transfer through land-purchase programmes, and the social security system. Most of it, however, goes out of Kuwait, through two channels: direct private and government purchase of goods and services through imports; and, secondly, through Kuwaiti foreign aid and private and government foreign investment. The private sector is responsible for very little productive economic activity. Its main concern is with the import of goods and services of all kinds as a result of the oil multiplier. Its second main activity is real estate, which is highly inflated by government policy.

9

This is a true picture of a consuming economy, and the problem is that this process has been going on for more than thirty years without any significant structural change in the economy.

Apart from the oil sector, the whole economy is suffering from two important problems. The first is the imbalance in imports and non-oil exports, always closed by the oil sector through government expenditure. The contribution of the non-oil sector to government revenue is negligible – about 3 per cent of total government revenue – and is mainly derived from import duties.

The second problem lies in the high percentage of foreign workers in the labour force. Any country's population is a basic determinant of its economic growth. The population of Kuwait was 206,473 in 1957, some 321,621 in 1961 and, according to the last census (April 1975), the population had increased to 994,837.

The foreign element formed 53 per cent of the total population and more than 77 per cent of the labour force, a very high dependence on foreign labour. Foreigners enjoy relatively free education and medical care – in the same way as Kuwaitis. However, they lack a sense of community, which might lead to social, economic and political difficulties. Also they are denied Kuwaiti nationality as a result of very strict nationalization laws. Further, they are taxed by Kuwaiti citizens and not by the government, as a result of the laws of commerce and commercial registry.

These two problems shed doubts on the ability of the economy to grow. The viability of the whole economy is highly questioned. Remove the oil sector and everything else will collapse. The state of conspicuous consumption through imports will stop; the schools will be without teachers; the hospitals will be without equipment, nurses and doctors; the foreign labour force will go back home; and probably the Kuwaitis themselves will have to leave Kuwait because they cannot go back to their old industries of seafaring and pearl-diving.

Effective, efficient government management, however, coupled with national economic policies, will be able to assure continuous economic prosperity. It is not the natural resources that build a nation but its people and their determination. Nevertheless, natural resources are important national assets and they must be protected by appropriate economic policies. It is with this insight into the future that this book is written. In the past, Kuwait's main national assets were its accessibility from the sea and the hard work of its people. It is now passing through a transitional period utilizing one of the most important assets in the world – oil – which will soon be depleted. Has the government of

Kuwait and its people prepared the ground for the shape of the pro-oil economy? It is the answer to this question with which the future parliament should be concerned. This book urges the Kuwaiti policy-makers to be aware of the consequences of being dependent on a depletable natural resource. They must seize the present opportunity of capital surplus to plan both for the near future and for further ahead.

Chapter 1

The pre-oil economy of Kuwait

Before the discovery and export of oil, the Kuwaiti economy depended on fishing, pearl-diving, seafaring, boat-building, herding and trade. These were the pillars of the Kuwaiti economy, from its establishment in the 1670s until the outbreak of the Second World War.

Fishing

The Kuwaiti diet relied mainly on fish from the Gulf. The Kuwaiti fishermen employed several methods of catching fish, each designed for the catch of a certain kind of fish at a particular place and time. For example, zubaidi was caught in shallow water between the islands of Failaka and Auhah and was caught using nets. The season for zubaidi lasted for five months, starting in December and ending in late April. During that period zubaidi constituted about 35 per cent of the total catch in Kuwait.

Other kinds of fish, such as the naqrur and newaibi, were caught by fishing line. Their particular habitat was between the island of Kubbar and the south coast of the mainland, and the season ran for three months, beginning in March and ending in May. During that period the yield of naqrur and newaibi represented some 40 per cent of the total catch of fish in Kuwait.

Shrimps were caught near Failaka Island during March and April and October and November, special triangular hand nets being used. During the months of October and November the catch of shrimps was 10 per cent of the total catch in Kuwait.

Other kinds of fish were caught by tidal weirs made of reeds and called hadrahs. They were built along the coast and used all the year round. Table 1.1 illustrates the above analysis.

Table 1.1 *Fishing catch in Kuwait by variety, method, season and geographical location*

Variety	Scientific name	Method employed	Season	Location
Shrimp		Hand net	March to April and October to November	Near Failaka Island
Zubaidi	*Pempus Argenteus*	Float net	December to April	Between Failaka and Auhah islands
Naqrur	*Pomadasys Argenteus*	Line	March to May	Between the island of Kubbar and the south coast of the mainland
Newaibi	*Otolithes Argenteus*	Line	March to May	
Others		Tidal weirs	All year round	

Source: J. G. Lorimer, *Gazette of the Persian Gulf, Oman and Central Arabia*, Calcutta, Superintendent Government Printing, 1908–15.

The nets and fishing boats were made in Kuwait by skilled workers. The reeds were imported from Iraq but the tidal weirs were made in Kuwait, especially by men from the Awazim and Reshideh tribes. These people made the tidal weirs, owned them, built them along the coast and managed them all the time. However, in certain cases the tidal weirs were owned by a merchant or a member of the ruling family but were managed by somebody else for a percentage of the daily catch of the tidal weirs.

The fishing sector of the Kuwaiti economy provided one of the most important occupations for the lower class in Kuwait. Wages and salaries were low. The fishing banks of Kuwait and its islands were capable of supplying Kuwait with more than 10,000 lbs (4,545 kg) of various kinds of fish a day during the early years of 1900.

The daily surplus of fish was usually dried and salted and was either exported to the interior or stored for local human and animal consumption. Zubaidi and shrimps were mostly sun dried and salted for future human consumption. In spite of the fact that more than 1,000 people from the coastal villages and towns of Kuwait were directly employed in fishing there was very little effort to develop the sun-dried and salted fish industry into a regular industry for export.

13

Pearl-diving industry

Pearl-diving is an old occupation of the inhabitants of the Arabian Gulf. Its profitability is subject to a high degree of uncertainty and its intricate working relationships are complicated and the consequent human sufferings are beyond repair. However, before an analysis of the industry and its role in the pre-oil economy of Kuwait is presented a brief description of its terminology and the parties involved is relevant.

(1) *Captain* He is called naukhada and is usually the owner of a pearl-diving boat or, most likely, the son of the owner. However, he is sometimes hired by the owner of the boat, who is an ordinary merchant. The naukhada is given full power to recruit his crew and is in command at sea.

(2) *Diver* He is called locally in Kuwait ghais. He is the man who dives into the sea and looks for the oysters on the sea bed. He is not equipped with any of the modern apparatus of modern-day divers, such as aqualungs. His only equipment is (i) a small knife to cut the oysters from the rocks of the sea bed; (ii) a clip made of wood, or from the horn of a mountain goat, which he puts on his nose; (iii) a basket, which he puts around his neck, in which to collect the oysters.

(3) *Hauler* He is called saib. He is always on the boat and his main function is to look after the diver by letting him down into the sea and by pulling him up from the sea bed.

(4) *Assistant hauler* He is called razif. His main function is to assist the hauler in all his work.

(5) *Tabbab* He is a boy younger than the razif. He does all sorts of things, according to his capabilities. However, he receives nothing at all except his food and the experience he gains.

(6) *Broker and middleman* The broker is called dallal and the middleman is called tawash. The tawash sometimes goes out to where the boat is operating and buys the pearls either for cash or in kind and sells them later at a much higher price.

The pearl-diving season started on 15 May and ended on 15 September. The captain (naukhada) began recruiting his crew long before the start of the season and in almost all cases he would take the same crew as he had in previous seasons. This was because of the system of financial debt built into the pearl-diving industry. The captain, by himself or on behalf of the merchants who owned the boat, made certain money advances to the crew. These advances were fixed by the merchants and with the approval of the Shaikh of Kuwait. (The shaikh's disapproval, however, did not oblige the merchants or the captains to increase the advances given to the crew. Nevertheless when the situation was very serious and the money advances very low the shaikh had a certain amount of leverage over the merchants through the threat that the crew might strike. It was in the interests of both the shaikh and the merchants that the pearl-diving industry continued uninterrupted year after year, for both stood to benefit financially.)

The money advances given to the crew, in order that they could look after their families and buy them the minimum essentials of food, were hardly sufficient to meet subsistence level. Consequently, this income was always supplemented by the wife, who provided domestic service at other people's houses. Further, the sons might be employed in the house-building trade and the daughters perform other kinds of domestic service as assistants to their mothers. The money advances were considered as liabilities against the crew and their families. This was especially true in the case of the divers and the haulers. After these advances had been accepted by the crew, the pearl-diving boats started their five months' journey.

The whole operation of the pearl-diving industry was open to a high degree of risk. In one season the boats might have a good catch in a good year when the price of pearls in the world market is high. On the other hand, they might have a very poor catch in a bad year when the price is low. Furthermore, good season or bad the distribution system on which the value of the catch was based was highly precarious. First of all, the crew did not attend, and had no say in, the sale of the pearls; they therefore had no real idea of how much the catch was sold for. Second, before the crew was paid the captain would deduct one-fifth of the value of the catch for himself, and he would then deduct from what was left the depreciation element for the boat and the cost of food, water and certain equipment carried in the boat. The remaining net value was then distributed among the crew. The result was always negative and therefore the divers and the haulers almost always received nothing. However, in the event that there was money left to be divided then a hauler received two-thirds as much as a diver, and the assistant hauler received half the hauler's share. As noted, the tabbab got nothing except food and experience of the job.

By the middle of September the season was over and the money advances that had been given to the crew for their families had already been used. However, they needed more money to feed their families and they therefore got further advances, known locally as tisqam, from the captain. These second money advances, which were supposed to keep the divers and their families at subsistence level until the next season, in effect tied the crew to their creditors and obliged them to go to sea next season. It was this built-in debt system that guaranteed the working of a labour force at subsistence level. If the divers and/or the haulers refused to go to sea the next season, for health or any other reasons, the result was tragic: the captain, either acting on his own behalf or on behalf of the merchants, would confiscate the house of the crew member and expel the family indefinitely.

Financially, the pearl-diving industry provided income for the merchants and the shaikh. The shaikh imposed a type of tax on the boats, the tax for each boat being equivalent to the advances paid for one diver. The merchants, apart from selling the pearls at good prices, accumulated capital through two further channels: first, they bought more boats and employed a large number of divers and haulers at a subsistence level; second, they acquired a large number of houses from crew members who were unable to pay their debts. It was this latter method of acquiring real estate that eventually allowed the merchants and captains of the pearl-diving industry to become extremely rich, via the land-assessment programme and urbanization scheme of Kuwait in the 1950s. The houses confiscated by the merchants during the pre-oil era were subsequently bought by the government at very high prices.

Finally, the pearl-diving industry was very hard and difficult as far as the divers and haulers were concerned. First, the divers were not allowed to eat or drink more than a very small portion of rice and dates. This was to keep them thin and thus enable them to dive quickly and to remain longer on the sea bed. Second, as a result of the above-mentioned diet the crew suffered from malnutrition and there was scurvy because of the lack of fruit and vegetables in their diet. Third, the absence of modern equipment meant that divers were readily and frequently exposed to attacks from sharks and stinging jellyfish. Finally, the continuous hot sun from May until September, together with the sea water and the lack of fresh showers after diving, caused a great deal of suffering and skin disease.

Pearl-diving was the main industry not only in Kuwait but throughout the whole Gulf region. Indeed, the Gulf was the major source of natural pearls in the world. At its peak, before the First World War, exports exceeded £2 million in value.[1]

In 1904 Kuwait had more than 500 vessels. More than 460 boats were engaged in pearl-diving, employing more than 9,000 men. A few years before the outbreak of the First World War the number of boats in the pearl-diving industry had reached 700 and the number of men employed had risen to 15,000. A large number of these men came from neighbouring countries and even from far-away countries such as Hadramount and Aden.

During the four months of the pearl-diving season the Kuwaiti pearling boats restricted their activities to the Gulf region (though they would go more than 100 miles south of Kuwait). During the winter months, however, when the climate in Sri Lanka (Ceylon) is not as cold as it is in Kuwait and the Gulf region, the pearl-diving boats would go to the pearl fisheries at Marichchukadi, close to Sri Lanka.

Probably the last visit to the banks of Sri Lanka was in 1925, because the Kuwaiti crews were bitterly disappointed with the results of their long trips and hard work. Their bitterness was accentuated because their catch had been small in previous years and the pearl market was not good. In the following year, 1926, the crews went on strike because of the low advances offered to them by the merchants and owners. Because of the small catch and the depressed markets for pearls in previous years the merchants were lacking capital or were not ready to advance enough money to persuade the crews to go to sea. The merchants were offering unbelievably small advances, to the extent that the crews were quite unable to accept them.[2] The Shaikh of Kuwait intervened and persuaded the merchants to pay more to the crews. The shaikh was finally able to persuade the merchants to pay 120 rupees per diver and 80 rupees per hauler.

By the start of the First World War the number of boats putting to sea was small compared with the pre-war years. The long and severe world depression after the First World War further decreased the number of boats putting to sea (Table 1.2). The introduction of the cultured pearl by the Japanese not only disturbed the price system of pearls, it almost killed the whole pearl-diving industry in the Gulf region. As a result, the number of boats putting to sea did not exceed 200, despite the availability of unemployed boats. The conflict between the crews and merchants in 1926 was repeated in 1931. The conflict was reinforced by the failure of the 1932 season, in which there were only 250 boats at sea whilst 350 remained idle.

Table 1.2 *The pearl-diving boats of Kuwait, 1900–45*

Year	Number of boats	Type of season
1900	550	
1901	552	
1902	450	
1903	453	
1904	450	
1905	461	
1906	470	
1907	550	
1908	650	
1909	670	
1910	680	
1911	700	
1915	600	
1916	500	
1917	480	
1918	328	
1919	328	
1920	325	
1921	320	
1922	225	
1923	400	
1924	450	
1925	475	
1926	200	Strike. Season worst on record
1927	200	
1928	300	On the whole, season successful
1929	600	Season good but catch down on previous year
1930	600	Complete failure
1931	650	Conflict between crews and merchants
1932	750	Big failure. Only 250 boats put to sea
1934	670	
1936	680	
1937	700	

Source: Lorimer, *op. cit.*, p. 1,053; administrative report of the Kuwait political agent, 1914–37; local sources of captains and businessmen; H. R. P. Dickson, *The Arab and the Desert*, Allen & Unwin, 1949, London, p. 484.

Seafaring and trade

As already noted the geographical location of Kuwait at the north-west tip of the Gulf gave it great economic, political and strategic importance. Its favourable position in relation to the main trade routes and its relative political stability have been major factors in its importance as a seafaring and trading centre.

The well-sheltered natural harbour of Kuwait and its proximity to the towns of Iraq and the Arab peninsula made it the main supplier to these towns. Its position as a link between the Persian and Arabian coasts of the Gulf, India and the Far East on the one hand, and the Mediterranean ports and Europe on the other hand, made it the best transit area for trade. It was the strategic geographical position of Kuwait that caused the major European powers – principally the British, French, Germans and Russians – to take such an interest in securing control in Kuwait.

Kuwait also attracted a number of merchant families from different tribes of the Arab Peninsula, for several reasons. First, the continuous wars among the tribes of the Arab peninsula made life difficult for the inhabitants of the towns and as a result many Arab traders looked to Kuwait as a peaceful town favourable to trade and stability. Second, the conflicts and wars between the Bani Khalid and the Wahhabi tribes caused a lot of destruction to the towns of the eastern part of the Arab peninsula and consequently many people of that region moved north and settled in Kuwait. Third, droughts occurred frequently and this pushed the Arab tribes toward the north and north-east of the Arab peninsula; some settled in Kuwait, whilst others continued north to Iraq.

The unsettled political situation in Persia during the eighteenth and nineteenth centuries, and the wars between the Ottoman empire and the Persians, encouraged numbers of trading families to move to Kuwait. As a result many Arab traders and inhabitants on the Persian shore of the Gulf settled in Kuwait. When the Persians besieged and occupied Basra between 1775 and 1779, Kuwait became the centre for the East India Company and consequently the company's staff moved out of Basra and were stationed in Kuwait. During that time the Wahhabi attacks on Kuwait were successfully repelled by the courageous townsmen of Kuwait.[3]

Basically, Kuwait provided transit trading services to Europe and the Far East. Its merchants owned the ships that carried cargo, materials and passengers and traded between Basra in the north and India and East Africa. The ships carried dates and grain to Kuwait and to the rest of the ports of the Gulf and India and East Africa. The pearl-diving industry provided highly valued pearls for export to Bahrain, whence the better pearls were sent to Europe whilst the inferior quality pearls were sent to India. On their return from India the ships carried wood, coffee, tea, pepper, spices, rice, iron and lead, and cotton yarn. Large quantities of these goods were carried by caravan to Baghdad and Aleppo.

The merchants and seamen of Kuwait benefited from the cargo and passenger trade to and from India. The Shaikh of Kuwait levied a 2 per cent import – purposely very low to attract trade from other ports of the Gulf. Although the income from such a low import duty might appear to be very small, the Shaikh of Kuwait had a further source of income from directing and protecting the desert caravans from Kuwait to Baghdad and Aleppo. En route, other Arab tribal chiefs received their reward in cash or in kind by providing their help to the caravans without interruption.[4]

It was the sea and land trade routes, coupled with the political stability of Kuwait, that made Kuwait a prosperous town, strong enough to defend itself. Table 1.3 shows that imports rose from Rs 710,000 in 1820 to Rs 4,818,929 in 1905. Similarly, exports rose from Rs 142,000 in 1820 to Rs 1,154,322 in 1905. During that period the number of sailing ships owned and employed by the Kuwaitis in high-sea trade increased from 35 to 86, and by 1932 it had reached 291. The average capacity of these ships also increased, from 250 to 300 tons, and in 1920 the total capacity of Kuwaiti seafaring ships was 140,000 tons.

Table 1.3 *Kuwait's foreign trade, 1820–1905*

	1820	*1905*	*1932*
Exports	Rs 142,000	Rs 1,154,322	
Imports	Rs 710,000	Rs 4,818,929	
Number of sailing ships employed	35	86	291

Source: Miscellaneous estimates, and reports on trade, British Political Agency, Kuwait.

In 1905 more than 30 per cent of Kuwait's foreign trade was with India. It consisted of imports of rice, tea, spices, coffee, sugar and piece goods. The Arab countries, under Turkish control, accounted for almost 27 per cent, made up of rice and grains and dates. The United Kingdom's contribution to Kuwait's foreign trade was 14.66 per cent, consisting of woollen materials and manufactured goods, arms and ammunition. There was also substantial trade with Persia, amounting to 9.21 per cent and composed of tobacco, barley and wheat. However, more than 18 per cent of Kuwait's foreign trade was with France and Germany, a large quantity of arms coming from France and quite substantial amounts of sugar cane coming from Germany. Trade directions and percentages are shown in Table 1.4.

Table 1.4 *Kuwait's foreign trade, 1905*

%	Country
30.75	India
26.77	Turkish Arabia
14.66	United Kingdom
9.21	Persia
18.61	France and Germany

Source: Reports on trade, British Political Agency, Kuwait, 1905.

Kuwait has grown rapidly over the years but unfortunately there are no reliable trade statistics. However, one could safely say that before the First World War the value of the Kuwaiti imports was less than Rs 6 million and the number of sailing ships owned, operated and managed by Kuwaiti citizens was more than 140. With the advent of the First World War Kuwait's foreign trade came almost to a standstill. The British government in order to control food and arms supplies from reaching Syria and other areas controlled by the Turks and the Germans, ordered the Shaikh of Kuwait, Shaikh Salem Mubarak Al-Sabah, to prevent the Bedouin caravans from buying food and/or arms from Kuwait. The shaikh did his best to oblige the British government but the British political resident in Kuwait was not satisfied with the measures taken and therefore asked the shaikh to supply him with the names of all the Kuwaiti importers together with the type and quantity of all the goods imported into Kuwait. The main reason for this was to secure full control of Kuwait's imports and exports. Nevertheless, large quantities of food and arms were smuggled in to Kuwait and then re-exported illegally into the interior of the Arab peninsula, Iraq, Syria and other areas controlled by the Turks. This smuggling made a few merchants very rich. The shaikh, however, lost a substantial amount of revenue through customs duties unpaid and some merchants were unable to market the goods they imported.

Matters were made worse, however, by the trade blockade imposed by King Abdul-Aziz Ibn Saud of Saudi Arabia, blocking all kinds of commodities entering Najd from Kuwait. He demanded that he should collect 7 per cent on all goods entering Najd via Kuwait and he even asked that one of his people should reside at the Kuwait customs office to collect the duties for him. All his demands were completely rejected by Shaikh Salem Mubarak Al-Sabah, and by his successor,

Shaikh Ahmed Al-Jaber Al-Sabah. (Shaikh Salem died on 27 February 1921. Shaikh Ahmed succeeded him, ruling until 1950.)

The blockade continued and military attacks were directed against Kuwait by the Ikhwan raiders. More than £11 million of damage was inflicted upon Kuwait. Further, the Great Depression was creeping in and several pearl-diving seasons had failed badly. Drought and famine in Najd in 1930 saw a number of members of different tribes from Najd allowed into Kuwait to buy supplies but that was not enough to revive the Kuwaiti trade. The tightness of the blockade and the successive failure of the pearling seasons in 1931 and 1932 reduced Kuwait and its population to great poverty and distress. People were leaving Kuwait, and many merchants had already left in 1930.

With the development of the oil industry in Iran beginning, Shaikh Ahmed Al-Jaber Al-Sabah, ruler of Kuwait, sold stones and sand from Kuwait to the Anglo-Persian Oil Company for its operation in Abbadan. The shaikh also introduced new taxes such as house tax, boat tax, motorcar tax, shop tax and slaughter-house tax. These measures were naturally very unpopular in Kuwait. However, Britain helped Shaikh Ahmed and Kuwait to consolidate its position. Britain exerted great pressure on King Abdul-Aziz of Saudi Arabia to relax his commercial blockade on Kuwait. The British Royal Air Force singled out the raiders on Kuwait and its vicinity and located and bombed them. Shaikh Ahmed also received help during the troubles of 1938, receiving advice from the British political agency in his handling of the demands for a constitutional government.

By this time the oil era had arrived, though the advent of the Second World War prevented full exploitation. Rationing of food was introduced and drought in 1940 made matters worse. Malnutrition was common, especially among the Bedouins, and tuberculosis killed many of them. Cards for rationing were distributed among families; however, without money they could not take advantage of their rationing rights. Some families had to make a month's rations last for three as a consequence. Nevertheless, with the end of the Second World War and the start of oil production and export the economic life of Kuwait changed dramatically, a change that has continued to this day.

Boat-building

As mentioned earlier, Kuwait was dependent on two main industries: pearl-diving and seafaring. The Kuwaitis built the ships needed by these two industries and, moreover, Kuwait became the boat-building centre for the whole Gulf. Many boats of different sizes and types were exported to the rest of the Gulf. Wood was imported from South East Asia and East Africa and the Kuwaiti carpenters designed the boats and built them. On average, more than thirty people were engaged in the building of a single boat, and the labour involved ranged from carpenters and assistant carpenters to ordinary workers and nail-makers, from weavers of sails to suppliers of lime, fat and paint.

On average, the Kuwaiti shipyards turned out more than 50 ships of different types and sizes annually. In 1931, which was not a good commercial year, the Kuwaiti yards produced 25 large pearling boats and 30 small fishing craft. It goes without saying that in good years the Kuwaiti yards were able to produce more than that. The average capacity of the seafearing ships ranged from 150 to 300 tons. In 1931 Kuwait was able to produce 4 cargo ships of an average capacity of 170 tons at a cost of Rs 35,000 each. In 1932 they were able to build a yacht of European design and 80 feet in length.[5]

The fishing, pearl-diving and seafaring industries were the bases of the Kuwaiti economy. The latter two industries were highly dependent on the state of the world economy. During depression years very few boats went to sea for pearl-diving and seafaring; consequently very few boats were built in Kuwait. The result was a decline in the income of the shaikh and the merchants, and an increase in the poverty of the working people. During boom years, however, Kuwait was always prosperous. More boats were built and more trade passed through its ports both for itself and for neighbouring countries. The Great Depression and the cultured pearl of Japan dealt a blow to the pearl-diving industry, and the trade blockade of Najd against Kuwait reduced to a minimum the number of seafaring ships that went to India and East Africa. The boat-building industry suffered greatly as a consequence. Its working force was soon absorbed by the oil economy in the years after the war.

Agriculture and herding

The climate of Kuwait is neither encouraging to herding nor inducive to agriculture. It is hot and dry, rainfall is scarce and is swallowed quickly by the sandy soil, and sand storms are a severe and not infrequent feature. Despite this the villages (such as Jahra, Fantas, Abu Halaifah and Dimna, now called Salmia) managed a variety of vegetables during the winter and summer months. The winter crops were tomatoes, egg-plant, chard, parsley, coriander, celery, cress, onions and white radish. The summer crops were water melon, melon, cucumber, pumpkin, okra, purslane and basil. The villages supplied almost all the demands of the town of Kuwait as far as vegetables were concerned. However, Kuwait imported all its grain and other agricultural products. A small amount of wheat and barley was grown at Jahra but more money was needed to develop and improve the land. Those with money to invest, however, were mainly concerned with fishing, pearl-diving and seafaring, and eventually, therefore, this small amount of wheat and barley culti-vation died out.

It is a well-known fact that among the nomadic Arabs wealth was counted and based upon the number of heads of sheep, camels, cattle and horses one had. Kuwait was no exception and herding served many purposes. First, it produced ghi, sheepskin, wool, specie and horses for export. Second, it kept the tribe together and supplied them with daily milk, butter and yoghurt, and on some occasions with meat. Third, the camels and horses were extensively used in war and were the main pillars of the army, for its mobility depended on the number and health of the horses and camels possessed.

Frequent drought and the spread of disease among the tribes took its toll. The drought of 1941 and 1942 was so severe that most people gave up any attempt to live in the desert and large numbers migrated to live in Kuwait town and the surrounding villages. However, conditions did not improve for them until after the war, when they were absorbed by the oil economy.

Population

Statistics on the size and distribution of the population of Kuwait before the oil era are scanty and whatever statistics are available were mainly derived from personal estimates of European travellers and/or the British Political Agency in Kuwait. Table 1.5 shows, as far as possible, the demographic evolution of Kuwait.

J. H. Stocqueler estimated the population of Kuwait to be 4,000 in-habitants in 1831. This figure does not include nomads and it is there-fore difficult to accept as accurate. A more reliable figure, however, is available for 1905, when the population of Kuwait had reached 35,000; it might well have been much more but for the epidemic of plague in

Table 1.5 *Population of Kuwait, 1831–1947*

Year	Population
1831	4,000
1905	35,000
1919	85,000
1947	120,000

Source: J. H. Stocqueler, *Fifteen Months Pilgrimage Through Introdden Tracts of Khuzistan and Persia in a Journey from India to England Through Parts of Turkish Arabia, Armenia, Russia and Germany in the Years 1831 and 1832*, London, 1832; Political Agency Report, 1910, 1918; White Leigh, 'Allah's Oil', in *Saturday Evening Post*, 20 November 1948.

1852. However, if the increase from 4,000 to 35,000 is accepted then an annual growth rate of more than 12 per cent is obtained. This was probably the case, for a number of reasons. First, a large number of people moved from Al-Hasa – the eastern part of present Saudi Arabia – to Kuwait. second, several merchant families moved from Zubara in Qatar to Kuwait, as a result of local tribal and religious conflicts. Third, a large number of people from the Persian coast crossed the Gulf and settled in Kuwait. Fourth, Najdi tribes, because of the fear of the Wahhabis (and later the Ikhwan), moved northward to the east and settled in Kuwait. Fifth, law and order coupled with stable prosperity and tolerance attracted people to settle in Kuwait. It would seem, therefore, that such an astonishing increase in the rate of growth of the population in the late nineteenth century need not be an exaggeration. It is similar to the growth rate for the post-oil era, which reached more than 13 per cent.

After 1905 the growth rate began to decrease, to 4.7 per cent annually. The population increased from 35,000 in 1905 to 85,000 in 1919. Of that total, 60,000 were residing in the town of Kuwait and 15,000 of them were of Persian origin. The remainder of the population was living in Kuwaiti villages (see Table 1.6).

The annual growth rate from 1919 to 1947 decreased and averaged a little more than 1 per cent. As Table 1.5 shows, the population increased from 85,000 in 1919 to 120,000 in 1947. In spite of the fact that no accurate information regarding the size and classification of the labour force is available one can state that almost every male individual more than 15 years of age was actively engaged in one job or another. There was seasonal unemployment because of the seasonal nature of the pearl-diving industry, which employed such large numbers of the population; however, this was mitigated by the building industry, which usually

Table 1.6 *Population of villages*

Village	Population
Jahra	500
Fantas	400
Abu Halaifah	200
Fahahil	200
Shiabeh	60

employed many of the crew members of the pearl-diving industry as a result of the low wages and availability of labour afforded by the off-season period.

The average wage level for a head mason was about Rs 5 in 1910 and for an ordinary worker or coolie it was about Rs 1. However, during the First World War the wage level almost doubled. A head mason received Rs 10, while an ordinary worker or coolie earned Rs 2 (see Table 1.7). The reason for this increase was the shortage of labourers in Kuwait as a result of better employment in Basra and Najd.

Table 1.7 *Wage rates before and after the First World War (in rupees)*

	1910	1918	1920
Head mason	5	10	10
Assistant head mason	2	5	7
Master carpenter	5	10	10
Assistant carpenter	2	5	8
Nail-driver	1½–2	3–4	6
Coolie	1	2	3

Source: Political Agency Reports, Administrative Report of Kuwait, Political Agency, 1917, 1918, 1919, 1920, 1921.

Chapter 2

Changing oil policies

The early years of oil in Kuwait, and in the Middle East in general, saw very favourable concessions to the oil companies. Concessions were exclusive in nature, were for long periods and covered large areas; concessionaires generally had a near monopoly and concessions were financed on a royalty basis, giving a limited cash return. As the importance of world oil, and in particular Kuwait's position within the global oil situation, became apparent there were increasing demands from within for Kuwait to take a more decisive role in her oil economy. Pressure from members of the Kuwaiti parliament and from certain areas of the Kuwaiti press brought issues to national prominence, highlighting issues on which it was felt that Kuwait had been the victim of a poor deal or had been badly treated, and presenting a series of demands to set matters right. Mounting pressure from these quarters and an increased awareness and greater experience in dealing in oil matters in general, particularly in negotiating with the oil companies, led to Kuwait acquiring a more appropriate control of her oil economies.

Issues of concern

Overproduction

From the beginning of drilling in the 1930s right up until 1970 there was no control over the operating practices of the oil companies. Companies could drill where they liked and could produce as much oil as they wished. Their objective was, naturally, to maximize the net total income in their home countries. However, in practice this meant that large quantities of oil were extracted from Kuwait over very short periods. Indeed, part of the Burgan field was damaged due to the quick

27

and high rate of oil production, causing the actual reserve-to-production ratio to decline by many years. As the daily oil production approached the technical limit of the oil wells in Kuwait, the reserve-to-production declined even further, resulting in a shorter life for Kuwait's only natural resource. At the same time, associated gas was flared and wasted, rather than put to good use.

Employment and training of Kuwaitis

It was increasingly felt that the oil companies were not honouring their commitment to the host country in terms of employment and training of Kuwaitis. Kuwaitis were not being trained or employed in highly important positions within the companies. It is true that Kuwaitis were employed by the companies — but as clerks, guards and drivers rather than as geologists, reservoir engineers, refinery engineers and petrochemical experts. Nevertheless, some were employed, having received their education in the USA and the UK, but not for very long because there were a number of constraints on their upward mobility. In brief, the companies were acting as foreign enclaves, as states within a shaikhdom, with one main objective: to supply the world market with cheap crude oil and to satisfy the shareholders whilst so doing.

Income from oil

British Petroleum and Gulf Oil Corporation in their concession in Kuwait were very much in the position of middlemen and brokers. As soon as oil began to flow to the world market British Petroleum agreed to sell Kuwaiti crude to Standard Oil Company of New Jersey and Mobil Oil Company, with whom it had agreements (signed in 1947 and 1948) for a quarter of a century. Likewise, Gulf Oil Corporation had a similar agreement with Shell to sell its share of Kuwaiti oil to the latter. Shell and Gulf Oil corporations agreed to share the profits on the sale of crude oil, its transport, its refining and marketing of the products. Kuwait itself could have done so, or at least should have demanded that part of the profits from downstream operations should accrue to the government. In selling a commodity, oil or otherwise, it has never been the case that a broker took more money than the owner of the commodity itself.

As a consequence British Petroleum and Gulf Oil Corporation were able to accumulate large profits. These profits were used to finance oil refineries and petrochemicals plants outside Kuwait. These industrial plants were built with almost 100 per cent bank financing, because the oil companies had full control on the source of crude oil. The same also applied to the building of oil tankers and terminals, which were again fully financed by the foreign banks merely because of crude availability to the oil companies. Consequently, no industry was built in Kuwait, and there was neither backward nor forward linkages to the oil industry in Kuwait. Kuwait could well have used capital for such purposes, thus avoiding, perhaps, many of the present bottlenecks in the Kuwaiti economy.

Expensing of royalties

It was only with the establishment of the Kuwaiti parliament that the issue of oil and gas became the focal point of internal and external politics. The first free parliament concentrated on the domestic practices of the oil companies and their financial payments to the Kuwaiti government.

During the first years of the Kuwaiti parliament the issue of the expensing of royalties was being discussed among the member countries of the Organization of the Petroleum Exporting Countries (OPEC) and the oil companies. The member countries of OPEC agreed to a discount equal to 12.5 per cent off posted prices in exchange for expensing of royalties at 12.5 per cent off posted prices. The Kuwaiti government, as a member of OPEC, accepted the same method of expensing of royalties adopted by the other members of OPEC. However, the Kuwaiti parliament rightly rejected it and refused to ratify it. The young parliamentarians in Kuwait could have accepted the Agreement of Expensing of Royalties if the oil companies would have agreed to drop the idea of discount off posted prices. Discount started at 12.5 per cent and gradually decreased to 6 per cent. Perhaps a numerical example will help illustrate the respective views of the oil companies, the Kuwait government and the Kuwaiti parliament.

(A) Let us assume that the posted price is $1.57 per barrel, the actual cost of production is 7 cents and the royalty is 12.5 per cent of posted prices. Accordingly, the income accruing to the Kuwaiti government will be as follows:

Posted price	1.57000
Cost of production	0.07000
Royalty at 12.5% of posted prices	0.19625
Cost of production + royalty as 12.5%	0.26625
Profit subject to 50% income tax	1.30375
Government's share	0.65187

In the above example the oil companies treated the item of royalty as an element of cost which was added to the actual cost of production before the net income was divided in half.

(B) The views of the Kuwaiti government and the oil companies after the latter accepted the expensing of royalties and the former accepted discounting of posted prices equal to 8.5 per cent:

Posted price	1.57000
Discount amounting to 8.5%	0.13330
	1.43670
Cost of production at 7 cents	0.07000
	1.36670
Royalty at 12.5% of posted price	0.19620
Profit subject to 50%	1.17050
Income tax at 50%	0.58520
+ royalty	0.19620
Government's share	0.78140

(C) The views of the Kuwaiti parliament — expensing of royalties but without discount off posted prices:

Posted price	1.57000
Cost of production	0.07000
Royalty at 12.5% of posted price	0.19620
Profit subject to 50% income tax	1.30380
Income tax at 50%	0.65190
Government's share (0.65190 + 0.19620)	0.84810

It is obvious from these figures that it is in the interests of Kuwait to accept the agreement of expensing of royalties but without discounts off the posted price, because the latter nullify the desirable effects of the actual expensing of royalties. It was thus that twelve members of parliament opposed the government and its agreement with the oil companies and refused to ratify it. The twelve members resigned as a consequence in December 1965.

By February 1966 the battle between the oil companies and the government on the one hand and the parliamentary opposition on the other had changed its arena from parliament to the national press. *Al-Tali'ah*, a leading national weekly journal that represented the views of the resigned members of parliament, started a systematic press attack in a series of articles. The main theme was the practices of the oil companies and the failure of the government to combat these. From 16 February until its suspension by the government in May 1966, *Al-Tali'ah* covered a number of important issues. It raised the issue of the actual cost of oil production, which was directly related to the expensing of royalties. This led to a wide discussion about the cost of production not only in Kuwait but also in the rest of the oil-producing countries of the Middle East. In all fairness, as far as this particular problem is concerned, *Al-Tali'ah* did not study the element of the cost of production well. Nevertheless, it raised a question to which neither the Kuwaiti government nor the oil companies wished to provide an answer. *Al-Tali'ah* estimated the cost of oil production in Kuwait to be 25 cents per barrel but the government insisted that the cost of production did not exceed 7 cents. In the end, however, this low figure for the cost of production was used neither by the government to solicit more concessions from the oil companies nor by *Al-Tali'ah* to plan for a more scientific press analysis and more sophisticated economic attack on the government.

Schedule of payments

During the four months of press attack by *Al-Tali'ah* on the oil companies and the government, the average man in Kuwait in particular and in the Gulf region in general was becoming interested in the writings of the journal on oil and gas affairs. In fact, it served as a public seminar on very important subjects. On 16 and 23 March 1966 *Al-Tali'ah* discussed two important issues.

The first issue was the marketing of oil products in Kuwait by the Kuwait National Oil Company (KNOC) rather than by Kuwait Oil Company, the latter owned by British Petroleum and Gulf Oil Corporation. KOC was making huge profits out of its sales of bunker fuel to oil tankers. *Al-Tali'ah* wanted that kind of sale to be handled by Kuwait's national petroleum company, especially because of the high frequency of oil-tanker traffic in the Gulf.

The second issue, which was covered rather slightly on 23 March, was the schedule of payments by the oil companies to the government. The schedule of payments was lagging behind oil exports by several months and the amount due to the Kuwaiti government was several hundred million dollars. The oil companies therefore were accused of making money out of the government's accumulated revenue, since they were thereby earning interest on it. In effect, the government was granting almost a year's credit to the oil companies and consequently was losing a year's interest on its capital and resources.

The last issue to be analysed by *Al-Tali'ah* was the currency of payment. The general practice of the oil companies at the time was to sell the oil in dollars but to pay the Kuwaiti government in Sterling. At the time, Kuwait's imports were increasing at a very fast rate from the USA, which led to a number of losses through currency conversions from Sterling back to dollars. This was during the heyday of the United States dollar; at the same time, Kuwait was accumulating large sums of Sterling, which were losing value as a result of inflation and Sterling devaluation in 1967.

After the systematic press attack on the oil companies and the government alike, the latter decided to clarify its position on the issues raised by the national press. The response of the Ministry of Oil, however, never clarified the government's position over these issues to any degree of satisfaction of its critics. Nevertheless, that exercise popularized the issues of oil and gas beyond the imagination of the parliamentary opposition, and Kuwait became, for the first time in history, a forum for a very important economic and political commodity. It was perhaps at this time that the government began to assume a more appropriate control of its oil economy.

The government waited until parliament was dissolved on 3 January 1967. New elections were called for on 23 January. The opposing members of parliament (those who had opposed the government over the expensing of royalties issue) lost the election and in May 1967, with the absence of the national opposition in the parliament, the new parliament ratified the Agreement of Expensing of Royalties in the form presented by the oil companies. As a *quid pro quo*, Kuwait Oil Company agreed that any dispute regarding Kuwaiti income tax should be under the jurisdiction of Kuwaiti national courts. The government had the right to inspect the production and operating costs of the activities of the past years. However, the most important item in the agreement as far as Kuwait was concerned was that the government could take the 12.5 per cent royalties either in kind or cash.

Kuwait National Petroleum Company

At this time plans for the construction of a refinery for Kuwait National Petroleum Company were in progress after the Economist Intelligence Unit reviewed the overall economics of the project. The economics of Kuwait National Petroleum Company were based upon a lack of product flexibility among the oil refineries of the world. There was a continuous shortage of oil by-products in the consuming countries because the pattern of consumption did not match the pattern of production by the existing refineries. Furthermore, the resulting shortage could not be relieved merely by expanding the capacities of the existing refineries. The most important shortage was kerosene in Asia and diesel and distillate heating oil in western Europe. Kuwait's geographical location between these two continents made it an ideal place to supply both markets.

Various western concerns reviewed the project from the viewpoint of an independent investor and, at the same time, the technical feasibility of the H-oil process was received, since the refinery was to employ a hydrogenation technique. Finally, various licensors were selected for different processes in the refinery.

So far so good. However, when KNPC received its refinery from the contractors there were immediate problems. The hydrogenation unit did not work for many years. The final production costs far exceeded the estimated costs of construction at Shuaiba. Worse than that, the feedstock to the refinery was bought from Kuwait Oil Company at an even higher price than the market price of Kuwait high-sulphur crude. Although Kuwait was entitled to take its royalty in kind, it did not do so, though this would certainly have been of great assistance to KNPC, which was, after all, the national oil company, in which the government held a 60 per cent share. It is unfortunate that the early years of KNPC were witness to such difficulties.

The benefits envisaged by the parliament from the Agreement of Expensing of Royalties were not realized. Finally, by the end of 1970 KNPC was approaching bankruptcy due to refinery closures, technical problems, higher prices for its crude input, and higher labour costs than any other refinery in the world. In spite of its monopoly in product marketing in Kuwait, it was only after the rising price of crude oil and its by-products, at the end of 1973, and the write-off of its previous losses, together with the complete takeover and ownership by the government, that KNPC was able to make a reasonable profit.

Gas utilization

At the end of 1969 and through most of the early years of the 1970s a major issue to be discussed in parliament was gas utilization. The oil companies flared several million cubic feet of gas a day, a fact that infuriated the Kuwaiti public in general and the Kuwaiti intelligentsia in particular, since they considered it a great waste. The government appeared reluctant to discuss gas utilization with the oil companies but found itself under concerted attack from the opposing members of parliament, who wanted full national control of gas and its utilization.

In July 1971 the Minister of Oil and Finance met in London with the executives of Gulf Oil Corporation and British Petroleum. It was explained that the Kuwaiti government wished to avoid a collision course with its parliament and that therefore the issue of gas utilization could not be ignored. In fact, it was repeatedly explained that unless a solution could be arrived at the parliament would pass legislation to nationalize the gas industry in Kuwait.

The oil companies did not appear to give these issues their serious consideration and their political analysts failed to predict the moves of the Kuwaiti parliament — they thought it a vehicle with no real power. The London meeting brought no solution. When the Kuwaiti parliament reconvened after the summer vacation on 28 October, the discussion of gas utilization continued. However, the Kuwaiti parliament wished to deliberate no further on the gas issue and finally, therefore, the gas industry was *de facto* nationalized by order of parliament.

Participation

A major issue to be discussed at length in the Kuwaiti parliament was the level of participation in the assets of the oil companies. At the start the oil companies were willing to accept the oil-producing governments as partners with a low percentage. The oil companies considered themselves generous in this acceptance and thought it a nice cushion against a more revolutionary demand among the oil-exporting countries. However, the Kuwaiti parliament rejected the offer of the Kuwaiti government to accept 25 per cent participation in the assets of the oil companies in Kuwait and opted for a higher percentage.

The heated discussions that took place in the Kuwaiti parliament regarding the percentage level of participation influenced the rest of the Gulf's oil-exporting countries. The Kuwaiti parliament did not accept, from the start, anything less than 40 per cent participation in the assets of the oil companies, which were to be compensated at book value, and therefore on 1 January 1974 the government acquired a 40 per cent share in KOC, so that the shares of British Petroleum and Gulf Oil Corporation stood at 60 per cent. By the end of 1976 KOC had become fully controlled by the Kuwaiti government and was retroactively taken over by the government with effect from 5 March 1975. The Kuwaiti parliament became the pioneer in that regard and history will record it for the enlightened parliamentarians who influenced and effected such decisions.

Production limits

We have already seen how overproduction was an issue of concern among the Kuwaitis. As far as any limit on oil production is concerned this was due to the Liberal member of parliament, Mr Abdula Al-Nibari. On 28 May 1974 he addressed the parliament on almost all issues related to oil, gas and finance; he concentrated, however, on oil production and oil reserves. He was the first member of the Kuwaiti parliament to talk at length and from a position of great knowledge and experience. He spoke first about oil reserves and their present estimates and the need for a clear policy of oil production. He then went on to demand a national policy regarding the development of human resources in the oil industry; and rightly so, for even after the government's full ownership of KOC the operations are still run by non-Kuwaitis. Third, he insisted on the national utilization of gas for industry and that it should be linked to a national industrial development plan. Fourth, he demanded that Kuwait's financial revenue should match its needs and that therefore Kuwait should not produce more than it needed for its current budget — Kuwait was losing a large amount of money in its portfolio investments as a result of rising inflation and currency depreciation. Oil in the ground is better than continuously depreciating cash.

The issues of oil reserves and oil production are interrelated and are very important as far as national planning is concerned. Kuwait's oil production reached more than 3,800,000 barrels a day by the end of

March 1972. Although the parliament had already set an upper limit on oil production — at not more than 3,000,000 barrels a day — neither the oil companies nor the government strictly followed the dictates of the national parliament. The government claimed that it interpreted the latter's decision to mean that only the oil production of KOC should not exceed 3,000,000 barrels a day. However, the members of parliament had, in their decision to set an upper limit on oil production, meant that limit to be for the total national oil production irrespective of the oil companies operating in Kuwait and the Neutral Zone.

The limit on oil production in Kuwait had far-reaching effects. It increased the shortage in world oil supply at a time when the world demand was increasing in general and the United States imports were accelerating in particular. Consequently, the actual price of crude oil in the open market became higher than the posted prices. Such a price structure had not occurred for many years; nevertheless it happened soon again in February 1979 as a result of the interruptions in oil supplies from Iran. The higher actual prices of oil in the world market, which exceeded posted prices in 1972 and 1973, strengthened the position of the member countries of OPEC, which led to even higher posted prices by OPEC. The Kuwaiti parliament's limit on oil production not only improved Kuwait's reserve-to-production ratio, it also helped the Kuwaiti government and other members of OPEC to realize higher oil prices for their depletable resources.

Much more important was that the major oil companies were no longer able to use Kuwait to balance oil demand and oil supply. In the 1950s and 1960s Kuwait was always relied upon by the oil companies to make up for the slack in oil supply that occurred as a result of technical and political problems. Whenever there was a situation to cause a stoppage or to produce a reduction in oil production in the Middle East, Kuwait's importance in alleviating the situation came to prominence. For example, in 1951 Dr Mussaugh of Iran tried to nationalize the oil industry, which caused a long stoppage in oil exports. Nevertheless world oil demand and supply were not badly affected because the oil companies forced an increase in oil production from Kuwait to compensate for the production losses from Iran. The same policy was followed in 1961 when General Kassim of Iraq had his quarrel with the oil companies. In brief, the low cost of oil production and the technical capabilities of the oil facilities to increase oil production easily and quickly, were the assets of Kuwait on which the major oil companies were dependent.

However, by the middle 1970s that situation had changed dramatically because of the oil ceiling imposed by the Kuwaiti parliament and the world-wide shortage of oil. Nevertheless, British Petroleum, Gulf Oil Corporation and Shell remained dependent on Kuwait oil production to meet their marginal needs. Other major oil companies and the rest of the oil industry became reliant on Saudi Arabia to meet their oil demand. From the middle of 1976 onwards Saudi Arabia was relied upon by the major and independent oil companies alike to meet their needs. That dependence became more evident during the Iranian oil crisis precipitated by the revolutionary processes in Iran in February 1979. Saudi Arabia assumed the role formerly played by Kuwait and will continue to do so for some years to come. Probably it will manage to meet the world demand for oil during the coming instability of oil supplies as a result of the present explosive political situation in the Middle East. However, if oil supplies are interrupted from Saudi Arabia itself, as a result of national demand or political instability, then there will be no other place in the world to make up for the Saudi oil losses, in spite of the very sophisticated logistics systems of the major oil companies.

Oil concessions and oil policy

The history of oil concessions in Kuwait dates back as far as 1911. In that year the managing director of APOC, Sir Charles Greenway, encouraged by the earlier discovery of oil in the Gulf area by APOC, and through the knowledge that Shell Oil Company was trying to obtain a concession, wrote to the British president, Sir Percy Cox, to obtain a concession in Kuwait.

Evidence of further British interest in Kuwait's oil possibilities came with the British government's decision to convert the Navy to oil-burning ships. Because of this a group of Admiralty experts was sent to Kuwait to conduct a survey. The group visited the Hills of Burgan, where the seepage was clearly marked, indicating what was later to be the location of the biggest oil-field in the world.

A geological survey was undertaken by APOC in 1914 but a further survey by APOC was delayed until 1917 because of the First World War and the death of Shaikh Mubarak Al-Sabah. After its brief survey at Burgan, south of Kuwait town, and at Bahra, north of the town, the company decided upon a vigorous but cheap oil concession. However, as a result of the peace settlement of the First World War and the break-up of the Ottoman Empire little happened until the early 1920s. In 1922 APOC put forward its proposals for a concession to the new shaikh, Shaikh Ahmed Al Jaber Al-Sabah, but whilst he was considering these proposals he received an alternative offer from a Major Frank Holmes, representing Eastern & General Syndicate Ltd (EGS). Holmes was one of the great concession hunters of his time. He had obtained an exclusive option for oil exploration in Saudi Arabia from King Abdul Aziz Ibn Saud. No sooner had he signed it than he planned to gain an oil concession in Kuwait. Consequently he cabled Shaikh Ahmed from Bahrain telling his highness about the oil concession from King Abdul Aziz Ibn Saud and asking him to wait and not to conclude any agreement with any other company before he was acquainted with his terms.

On 25 May 1923 Holmes arrived in Kuwait and presented his terms to Shaikh Ahmed. Though Shaikh Ahmed was able to see the better terms of Holmes's offer he was nevertheless reluctant to accept it because it was not sanctioned by the British government. His reluctance was due to the 1899 agreement with Britain and a letter of reply to the British political representative, Sir Percy Cox, in 1913, from Shaikh Mubarak who thereby agreed not to give a concession to anyone who was not nominated by the British government.

Negotiations continued in a rather haphazard way until 1926. By this time EGS had outstretched itself with interests in this area and it offered its interest in the Gulf area to APOC. APOC declined but Holmes secured the interest of Gulf Oil in the USA and in 1927 Gulf Oil bought all the interest of EGS in the Gulf area. This completely transformed the situation since there were now two major oil companies involved, with the backing of their respective powerful governments.

In 1928 the British government informed Holmes that they would require a British Nationality clause in any agreement he made with the shaikh. This was also made a condition of EGS's Bahrain concession, though it was later removed for the latter concession. When it was not also removed for the Kuwait concession the US government was brought in and after much pressure the British government decided to waive the nationality clause. This was in April 1932. The Foreign Office agreed 'to the omission from any oil concession which the Shaikh may be prepared to grant, of a clause confining it to British interests.' The US ambassador to Britain was Mr Andrew Mellor, the principal owner of Gulf Oil.

Negotiations were continued and proposals were put to the shaikh from both APOC and Gulf. However, by early 1933 the two companies had decided on co-operation and in May 1933 formed Kuwait Oil Company (KOC) with a capital of £50,000. It was KOC that was thenceforth to negotiate with the shaikh.

At this time a new, wholly British, company called Traders Ltd made an offer for a concession. Several influential British businessmen and important political figures, were behind Traders Ltd, and it was a reaction to US intervention in the Gulf region through Gulf Oil Corporation. The offer from Traders Ltd precipitated an acceptance from KOC of the shaikh's terms. Traders Ltd in fact gave better terms but despite this the shaikh declined and on 23 December 1934 Shaikh Ahmed Al Jaber Al-Sabah signed the first oil concessions with KOC.

An economic appraisal of the KOC concession

Before KOC achieved its oil concession in Kuwait, there were oil concessions in Saudi Arabia, Iran and Iraq. In spite of this fact, royalty payments to Kuwait were lower than those to these other countries. The rate they were paid was 22 cents a barrel; Kuwait was given 13 cents a barrel, which came to 9 cents a barrel after the Sterling devaluation of 1949. Other concessions in Iraq, Iran and Saudi Arabia were not affected by Sterling devaluations because they had insisted on a gold clause in their agreements with the oil companies.

The area covered by the concession is very large compared with leased areas in the western hemisphere. In Venezuela, for example, the area given to the oil companies for exploration does not exceed 38 square miles, whereas the Kuwaiti concessions cover almost the whole of Kuwait and its islands (except Kubbar). This effectively means that it is not necessary for KOC to enter into excessive competitive activities. It can shift its drilling from one well to another whenever it finds the cost of production rising. By doing this KOC is spared all the costs of loss of gas pressure and oil recoverable from its oil-fields. Two financial results are relevant: first, KOC can always achieve a high output per well; second, it can always accelerate the rate of oil production without increasing production costs, because it does not need to drill deeper and deeper in one well.

It is always easy for the company to move to another well or another field. Legally, KOC is not restricted by laws of conservation; that is why it is always free to shift its drilling sites. The concession agreement between KOC and Kuwait does urge KOC to 'use the most appropriate scientific methods'. Nevertheless, it does not specifically state conservation obligations.

The duration of the KOC concession in Kuwait is the longest on record — 92 years. Its significance is very clear if it is compared with the concession duration of neighbouring countries. In Iran the period of concession is 40 years, in Iraq it is 75 years, in Saudi Arabia 66 years. Oil exploration and production requires a fairly lengthy duration; it is very rare for a commercial discovery to be made in less than three years from the concession being granted. However, the length of the KOC concession is generous beyond imagination.

In 1951 profit-sharing agreements were introduced in Kuwait after their adoption by Saudi Arabia in 1950. The main reason for this was the tax credit of the parent country. Since 1939 the US government has offered a tax incentive in the form of a percentage depletion allowance. It is applied by exempting 27 per cent of the gross income from income tax. Although the British government does not offer a depletion allowance, it does give income-tax credit. These tax-credit advantages could have influenced the oil companies and in this case KOC to introduce the 50–50 profit-sharing a long time ago. However, KOC was reluctant to change the fiscal terms of the concession because it might lead to radical changes. Moreover, the absence of income-tax legislation in Kuwait was a great encouragement to KOC not to introduce the principle of a profit-sharing scheme. On the Kuwaiti government side, the lack of well-versed negotiators in the techniques of international economics, finance, law and industry, was a major obstacle.

However, the profit-sharing agreement eliminated royalties — in other words the payment of 50 per cent of the profit of crude-oil production to Kuwait included royalties, rents and income-tax receipts. In brief, and in accounting terms, the royalties were not expensed. Nevertheless, the oil companies agreed later on (during 1967) to expense royalties, but asked for a discount of 6.5 per cent off posted prices. The Kuwaiti parliament ratified the new agreement of expensing of royalties, which brought the tax collection up to 85 cents a barrel.

Finally, KOC evaded the implementation of the 'Equal Treatment with Iraq' clause in its agreement with the Kuwaiti government. In a letter dated 30 December 1951, KOC addressed His Highness, the Amir, as follows:

If in the future, the Iraq government receives a greater percentage of profit, the companies (here the parents of K.O.C. which are B.P. and Gulf) will be willing to review and discuss the situation with Your Highness in the light of the new Iraq terms and all other relevant facts and circumstances.

The content of that letter was confirmed in Article 1 of the agreement of 11 October 1955. However, Iraq continued to receive a higher percentage of profit than Kuwait; the clause of equal treatment with Iraq was completely ignored and was never implemented.

To account for the percentage profit received by Kuwait and Iraq, three variables should be studied: the cost of production; the price of exports; and the percentage figure. The cost of oil production in Kuwait was very low compared with any other oil-producing area in the world. The lifting costs in Kuwait never exceeded 10.5 cents a barrel and it went much lower during the 1960s. It reached as low as 6.1 cents a barrel. In Iraq, as stated in Article 9 of the 1953 agreement between Iraq and Iraq Petroleum Company, the cost of production was 13 shillings a ton (about 24 cents a barrel). As to the difference in export prices, it was generally believed that Kuwait prices were artificially deflated in comparison with Iraq.

If one uses the standard method of computing the taxable profits of oil companies in Iraq and Kuwait, then it will show that Kuwait (which was receiving oil revenues amounting to 50 per cent of the profits) was in fact getting less than Iraq, for Iraq was getting a higher percentage of profit than Kuwait. In Kuwait, income tax was based upon a weighted average price per ton of crude oil, while in Iraq income tax was based on posted prices. Two important points were relevant as a result of the different basis on which income tax was calculated in the agreements between the oil companies and the governments of Kuwait and Iraq. First, between 1951 and 1955 the market for crude oil was a sellers' market with spot cargos selling at higher prices than cargos on long-term contracts. Second, as a result of the first point the weighted average price per ton was much lower than the posted price. On the basis of these two points, the Kuwaiti government was receiving a smaller percentage of the profit than the government of Iraq. Needless to say, the Iraq agreement was subsequent to the Kuwait agreement. The former was dated 3 February 1952, the latter 30 December 1951.

An economic appraisal of the neutral zone oil concession

The neutral zone comprises about 2,000 square miles of settled land disputes but with an unsettled off-shore area between Kuwait and Saudi Arabia. The land is divided into two equal portions and is rich in oil resources. At present it is exploited by two companies: the American Independent Oil Company (Aminoil) and the Getty Oil Company. The former works for Kuwait and the latter Saudi Arabia. However, for convenient reasons both companies have a joint operation in the neutral zone. The Kuwait-Saudi Arabia off-shore neutral zone is exploited also by the Japanese Arabian Oil Company, owned by a number of Japanese industrial interests.

Aminoil

Aminoil is the second concessionaire operating for Kuwait. On 28 June 1945 His Highness Shaikh Ahmed Al Jaber Al-Sabah granted a concession to Aminoil for 60 years. This agreement limited Aminoil operations to the on-shore neutral zone. However, on 22 September 1949 the area of the concession was extended to include the islands of Kubbar, Qaru and Umm Al-Maradim, and the territorial waters of these islands extending to three nautical miles.

In comparison with the KOC concession the Aminoil concession is a better deal for Kuwait in terms of payment accrued to the government, duration of concession and the size of the area under concession. By the 1948 concession Aminoil paid a royalty of $2.5 per long ton of crude oil produced and paid a tax-exemption fee of 7.5 cents per ton won and saved. KOC used to pay 13 cents and a tax-exemption fee of 4 annas per long ton of crude oil won and saved.

Aminoil gave a bonus of $7.25 million for its concession, while KOC paid about $178,000 followed by an annual rent of about $94,000 on discovery of oil. Aminoil made a minimum annual payment of $625,000 and 15 per cent 'carried interest' or share of net profits. KOC paid no such carried interest and made a much lower payment despite the fact that the oil-fields of KOC are the most prolific in the world.

When the agreement with Aminoil was modified in July 1961 an option was given to the government either to receive 57 per cent of realized profits or 50 per cent of the profits based on posted prices, the government to take whichever was the higher. The amounts due were to be discharged by the payment of a royalty of 12.5 per cent of the posted price and Kuwait income tax. In 1967 Aminoil agreed to expense royalties but asked for a discount of 6.5 per cent of the posted price.

The size of the area under the Aminoil concession is smaller than KOC and the duration of the concession is shorter. The geological structure of the area under KOC concession is much more favourable to oil exploration and production than Aminoil. However, comparison of Aminoil payments to the Kuwaiti government with those of its partner, Getty Oil Company (the holder of the Saudi Arabian share of the concession in the Neutral Zone), reveals that the Kuwaiti government received 43.6 cents per barrel from Aminoil in the years 1967-8, whilst the government of Saudi Arabia received 76.2 cents per barrel from the Getty Oil Company, in spite of the fact that there was no difference in the quality of the oil produced by the two companies.

The Arabian Oil Company

A concession in the off-shore area of the Neutral Zone was granted by Saudi Arabia to the Arabian Oil Company in 1957. Kuwait also made an agreement with the same company to produce and refine the oil in the same area. The agreement was signed in May 1958, one year after the Saudi Arabian agreement.

In comparing the concession of the Arabian Oil Company with Aminoil or KOC, the government seems to have gained a better deal with the Arabian Oil Company — a result of their increased experience in negotiation of oil concessions. The duration of the concession, as stated in Article 2 of the agreement, is 44.5 years effective from 5 July 1958. This is shorter than that of either KOC or Aminoil.

In terms of the place and currency in which Kuwait's dues are paid the Kuwaiti negotiators have again fared better with the Arabian Oil Company than they did with KOC and Aminoil. Article 34 insisted that all payments due to the shaikh should be paid in US dollars to accounts designated by the shaikh in writing. This was in direct contrast to KOC, which paid in Sterling. The dollar is the nearest currency one can have to an international means of payment and standard of value.

The Arabian Oil Company pays the Kuwaiti government 57 per cent of the profits made by the company at all stages of oil operations, which includes crude-oil production, refining, transport and marketing. KOC and Aminoil pay mainly for one stage, i.e. crude-oil production.

The royalty paid by the Arabian Oil Company is higher than the royalty paid by KOC and Aminoil. It pays 20.5 per cent of the posted price of oil won and saved. The other companies pay only 12.5 per cent.

The Arabian Oil Company is only one in which there is state participation (that is, of course, before the government takeover of KOC). Article 12 of the agreement between the Kuwait government and Arabian Oil Company states that after the discovery of oil in commercial quantities the Kuwaiti government has the right to 10 per cent of the shares of the company at the original issue price.

Chapter 3

The role of the oil sector in social and economic development

Methodology

The methodological issue is one of how to evaluate the role of the oil sector in the economic development of Kuwait. Such an evaluation is made possible through the analysis of available data, which allows the relative importance of different contributions from the oil sector to be shown. Each contribution represents a channel or an economic variable contributing to the growth of the whole economy. These contributions can be grouped into three basic categories: product; factor; and market.

1 Product contribution

This kind of contribution will deal with two aspects of product: (1) the increase of product in the oil sector itself; and (2) the increase of output of the oil sector as an increase in the gross national product of Kuwait.

2 Factor contribution

This kind of contribution will deal mainly with the transfer of capital and of labour. As far as capital is concerned, there are two kinds of capital transfer. The first kind is that from the oil sector to the government by royalty payments and taxation, and recently by government direct sales of crude oil, liquefied petroleum gas and refined products. The second kind of capital transfer is from the government to the whole economy through land-purchase programmes, expenditure on social-overhead capital, development projects and social transfers.

As to labour transfer, it is the growth of the population in general and the labour force in particular. Domestic and foreign labour was attracted by a higher wage gravity emanating from the oil sector as well as through government policy.

3 Market contribution

The market contribution of the oil sector will trace the development and size of economic activities nationally and internationally. The development of national banks, investment and insurance companies and other service activities will be the domestic-market contribution. The growth of international trade originating from oil exports and the imports of food, capital equipment and other materials will trace the international aspect of the market contribution of the oil sector.

Product contribution

1 Oil production

Since the beginning of the first commercial oil export in Kuwait in 1946, up to the end of 1965, the oil sector had been increasing its production at a rate faster than average for other oil-exporting countries. This was due mainly to the low cost of oil production in Kuwait, and as oil production increased the unit cost decreased, which led to great economies of scale. Favourable geological formations and the terms of the oil concessions also contributed to the low cost of oil production.

Table 3.1 demonstrates the high rate of growth in the oil sector. From 1951 to 1958, however, the rate of increase slowed down to an average of 15 per cent, although Kuwaiti oil production was still rising at a higher rate than any other oil producer. From 1958 to 1963 the rate of increase dropped to an average 8 per cent. The reason for this slowing down was mainly the decrease in crude-oil prices in 1959 and 1960, a decrease opposed by the oil-producing countries.

The oil companies regarded this reduction as potentially dangerous. To solve the problem, the oil companies began to increase oil production in the big oil-producing countries, to offset the losses they suffered from price reductions. However, in order to keep their production of outlet capacity in balance, the oil companies had to reduce oil production in small oil-producing countries such as Kuwait and Qatar.

During the period 1962–4 oil production increased by 10 per cent annually. There were two reasons for this increase. First, when General

Table 3.1 *Total crude-oil production of Kuwait, 1946–77 (millions of barrels a year)*

Year	Oil production	% change
1946	5.9	–
1947	16.2	174.5
1948	46.5	187.03
1949	89.9	93.33
1950	125.7	39.8
1951	204.9	63
1952	273.4	33.4
1953	314.6	15
1954	349.8	11.18
1955	402.8	15.5
1956	405.5	0.67
1957	424.8	4.75
1958	522.4	23
1959	525.9	0.67
1960	619.2	17.74
1961	633.3	2.27
1962	714.6	12.83
1963	765.2	7.08
1964	842.2	10.06
1965	861.5	2.3
1966	906.7	5.24
1967	912.1	0.6
1968	956.2	4.81
1969	1,011.7	5.8
1970	1,090.6	7.8
1971	1,166.4	7
1972	1,201.6	3
1973	1,102.5	– 8.3
1974	929.4	–15.7
1975	760.7	–18.15
1976	785.0	3.09
1977	718.1	– 8.5

Source: Ministry of Oil, Kuwait, 1978.

Qassim of Iraq issued his famous Decree No. 8 in 1961, which implied the expropriation of areas of concession under the Iraq Petroleum Company, oil production was suspended temporarily. This event led KOC to increase its production in Kuwait. Second, in 1962 the Arabian Oil Company entered its second year of oil-exporting in Kuwait. Its rate of growth was highest in 1962.

In 1965 and 1966 the rate of growth increased by only 2.3 per cent and 5.2 per cent respectively. This low rate of growth is attributed to the increase in oil supply from Libyan and Nigerian fields. In 1967 the rate of growth sank very low. This low rate of growth is attributed to the Arab-Israeli War. However, during that year the Arabian Oil Company was increasing its production and was permitted to export all its production to Japan, which was not on the list of boycotted countries. If it were not for the production of the Arabian Oil Company, the rate of growth would have fallen to less than 0.3 per cent.

After the boycott ended, the rate of growth of the oil sector began to increase. The average annual increase during the period 1968-72 was 5.68 per cent. Nevertheless, the pressure of domestic public opinion was demanding a policy of oil and gas conservation, which culminated in parliamentary legislation to limit oil production to 2 million barrels a day. In fact, even that rate is very high in relation to Kuwait's foreign-exchange needs to finance government local expenditure.

The eruption of the 1973 Arab-Israeli War gave the government of Kuwait the opportunity to reduce oil production as a result of its oil-boycotting policy. In subsequent years and up to the end of 1975 oil production was decreasing at a very high rate in order to maintain the prevailing level of crude-oil prices in support of OPEC oil policy. By the end of 1975 production of oil had dropped by more than 40 per cent in comparison with the 1972 figures. The only increase in this period was in 1976, when oil production rose by 3.09 per cent as a result of increasing world demand in the second half of the year because of fear of rising prices for crude oil in 1977. However, the general decrease in oil production in this period did not lead to a decrease in government oil revenue. On the contrary, the government received more oil revenue from 1973 onwards as a result of higher oil prices, the implementation of the participation agreement and, finally, the complete takeover by the government of the remaining interests of British Petroleum and Gulf Oil in KOC.

By the end of 1977 crude-oil production had declined again, by 8.5 per cent in comparison with the previous year. There were several factors behind the decline. First, there was the awkward two-tier price system which developed as a result of the Doha Conference in December 1976. During that conference some members of OPEC followed a 10 per cent increase in posted prices while others led by Saudi Arabia imposed only a 5 per cent increase. Kuwait was a member of the first group and demanded a 10 per cent increase in posted prices. As a result there was less demand for Kuwaiti crude oil in favour of less heavy crudes. A second factor was that the decision regarding the unsettled crude-oil price differentials put Kuwaiti crude in a disadvantageous position in the world market. It made Kuwaiti crude much more expensive in relation to other heavy crude oil. These two main factors were reinforced by a world demand for using lighter crudes dictated by technical, market and environmental factors.

2 Product contribution of the oil sector to the GNP

The national income accounts of the oil-exporting countries tend to underestimate the real contribution of the oil sector to their GNPs for political reasons. However, by so doing, these countries usually get a deceptive picture of their economies. The national income account of Kuwait greatly underestimates the contribution of the oil sector to Kuwait's economy. The estimate was put at 61.5 per cent of GDP for the year 1966-7 and 70 per cent for the year 1975-6. With regard to the method used in the calculation of the value added by the oil sector three major points should be made. First, the oil exports are calculated at posted prices rather than at actual realized prices. This inflates the value of the oil exports by a factor ranging from 5 per cent to 15 per cent. In the past, the oil companies sold their oil at a discount which sometimes reached 20 per cent of the posted price. The second point is that the use of the concept of GDP is conceptually irrelevant to the real contribution of oil to the Kuwaiti economy. By definition the GDP includes the inflated profits of the foreign oil companies, which do not accrue to Kuwait and have no economic effect on the Kuwaiti economy. The third point to be made is that the GDP concept excludes profit from Kuwaiti capital abroad, which has become substantial, especially since 1973 due to high prices of crude oil. Over the coming few years it will be almost equal to the revenue from oil exports.

Factor contribution

1 Labour transfer

The development of the oil industry in Kuwait brought with it a huge increase in population. The early years had seen a decline in the numbers employed in the old industries such as seafaring and pearl-diving, as a result of higher wages in the oil sector but also through the introduction of the cultured pearl from Japan and the development of more efficient sea-transport systems. With the rise of the oil industry, the majority of the labour force was attracted from neighbouring countries. The absorption of immigrants by the non-oil sector demonstrates the labour factor contribution to the whole Kuwaiti economy. The population of Kuwait increased from 120,000 in 1946 to more than 200,000 in 1957. The non-Kuwaiti element as given by the 1957 census was 45 per cent of the total population. Table 3.2 shows that during the second official census in 1961 the total population increased to more than 321,000.

Table 3.2 *Total population and labour force statistics*

Indicator	1957	1961	1965	1970	1975
Total population	206,473	321,621	467,339	738,662	994,837
Kuwaiti element	113,622	161,909	220,059	347,396	472,088
Kuwaiti element as %	55	50.3	47.1	47	47.5
Non-Kuwaiti element	92,851	159,712	247,280	391,266	522,749
Non-Kuwaiti element as %	45	49.7	52.9	53	52.5
Illiterates as % of Kuwaiti nationals	59.7	48.7	54.1	47.2	44.6
Illiterates as % of non-Kuwaitis	49.4	42.8	39.5	32.8	28.9
Total labour force	80,288		184,297	242,197	304,582
Labour force as % of total population	38.9		39.4	32.8	30.6

Source: Central Statistical Office, Ministry of Planning, Annual Statistical Abstracts, 1977, State of Kuwait.

The percentage of non-Kuwaiti citizens increased to 49.7 per cent of the population. By 1975 the population of Kuwait had reached 994,837 and the non-Kuwaiti element had increased to almost 53 per cent. The increase in the total population of Kuwait was due to both the influx of immigrants and to the increasing birth rate and decreasing death rate as a result of prosperity and better health conditions among the Kuwaitis. Another factor was the increasing number of Bedouins becoming naturalized Kuwaiti citizens.

The transfer of labour from neighbouring countries to the whole economy implies an important capital contribution to Kuwait. The reason is that almost all the immigrants are of working age and come to posts in Kuwait requiring education and training. They are a vital part of the Kuwaiti economy. Table 3.2 shows the level of illiteracy among non-Kuwaitis to be much lower than that among Kuwaitis. By the end of 1975 the immigrants were increasingly accompanied by their families, most of whom were not working and were, therefore receiving a large proportion of the social-services budget, provided almost free by Kuwait. According to the population census of 1975 the total labour force was 304,582 working individuals, which is 30.6 per cent of the total population. However, the non-Kuwaiti element in the total labour force reached 69.84 per cent, which is very high by any standard. The labour contribution of the non-Kuwaiti element far exceeds that of the Kuwaiti citizen in every economic activity in Kuwait. However, the dominance of the foreign labour force is more greatly felt in the services sector, including the government sector.

2 (a) Capital transfer from the oil sector

The second transfer factor is capital. This accrued to the government directly from the oil companies. As reflected in Table 3.3, the money received by the government, which included taxes and royalties, was coming in at an increasing rate from 1946 up to 1976–7, with the exception of 1949 when there was no exact correspondence between oil exports and oil revenue received from KOC, the only company operating in Kuwait at the time. The decline in payments in 1949 was due to the devaluation of the Indian rupee, which followed the devaluation of the pound Sterling. The ruler of Kuwait was paid in rupees and consequently he suffered after devaluation. However, it is interesting to note that Iraq was not affected by devaluation even though its currency was linked to the pound Sterling. This was because Iraq had insisted on a gold clause in their dealings with the Iraq Petroleum Company.

After 1949 payments received by the ruler continued to increase. This was due to (1) increased oil production (2) the introduction of the 50–50 profit-sharing scheme in 1951, and (3) more recently to the increase in the posted price of oil.

The reason for the increased oil production was that after the nationalization of the oil industry in Iran in 1951, KOC increased its oil exports to take up the slack created by the cessation of Iranian

Table 3.3 *Government oil revenue, 1946–77 (KD thousands)*

Year	Amount	Change
1946	200	
1948	3,425	1,612.5
1949	2,950	– 16.10
1950	3,100	5.08
1951	7,500	141.93
1952	34,850	364.66
1953	60,161	72.62
1954	69,302	15.29
1955	100,498	45.0
1956	103,921	3.40
1957	110,161	6.0
1958	149,734	35.92
1959	146,843	– 1.93
1960	168,605	14.8
1961	164,702	– 2.314
1962	188,814	14.639
1963–4	198,772	5.27
1964–5	258,400	30.0
1965–6	279,180	8.04
1966–7	292,100	4.59
1967–8	293,500	0.48
1968–9	277,700	– 5.38
1969–70	291,600	5.0
1970–1	321,100	10.116
1971–2	500,900	56.0
1972–3	537,500	7.30
1973–4	584,000	8.65
1974–5	2,534,800	334.04
1975–6	2,793,300	10.02
1976–7	2,357,500	– 15.60

Source: Ministry of Finance, Kuwait, 1977

exports. This increase in oil exports from Kuwait was very important to British consumption because, if it were not for Kuwait and other Middle East oil producers, Britain would have paid in dollars for its oil imports at a time of dollar shortage. That state of affairs, together with rising world demand, increased the profits of KOC and the oil revenue received by the Kuwaiti government.

The second factor that added to the increase in revenue was the introduction of the 50-50 profit-sharing arrangement between the Kuwaiti government and KOC, effective from 1 December 1951. There were pitfalls in this agreement (for example, it eliminated royalties, because the latter could be charged against tax liability) but despite these the income received from KOC continued to increase.

As concessions were granted to other companies, to exploit Kuwait's oil resources in the Neutral Zone, oil revenues continued to increase. Aminoil and the Arabian Oil Company began to increase their payments as their production began to increase. This increase began to gain momentum in 1958. Despite the increase in oil exports, government revenue declined in 1959 and 1961. This was ascribed to the reduction of oil prices in February 1959 and August 1960. The first reduction amounted to 10 per cent of the posted prices while the second was equivalent to 6 per cent. Nevertheless, government receipts from the oil companies continued to rise in 1963-4, 1964-5, 1965-6 and 1966-7.

In addition to an increase in oil production and exports, the sharp rise in the percentage increase in 1964-5 was ascribed to a change in the method of payment by KOC. Prior to 1964, tax payments by KOC were lagging 15 months behind production. In April 1964 an agreement was reached between the government and KOC, in which tax payments were paid on the basis of the calendar years, 1963 and 1964. To solve the problem, it was agreed that the tax liability in oil production for the year 1963 should be divided into three instalments, to be paid in 1964-5, 1965-6 and 1966-7.

In January 1967 there was a sharp increase in oil production but after February 1967 the rate of oil production began to decline to the extent that the rate of increase in oil production for the year 1967 amounted to only 0.7 per cent. The sharp increase in January was due to the stoppage in mid-December 1966 of oil from Iraq to the Mediterranean through pipelines across Syria. Kuwait, as usual, picked up the slack in oil and increased its production. The flow of oil was resumed at the end of February 1967 after an agreement was reached between Iraq Petroleum Company and the Syrian government. The low rate of increase of oil production for the other half of 1967 could be attributed to the stoppage of oil exports from Kuwait to the USA, Britain and West Germany by the Arab-Israeli War of June 1967. Nevertheless, oil payments to the government did not decrease in proportion to the decrease in oil production. There were two reasons for this. First, the unit cost of oil production was decreasing, which meant an increase in oil companies' profits, which in turn added to the government's share of tax receipts. The second reason was changes in the terms of payment. As stated, before 1951 the 50-50 profit-sharing agreement used to treat royalty payments as a charge against tax liability. However, in 1966 an agreement was reached between the government and KOC (which was ratified by the National assembly in 1967) which provided the treatment of royalty payments on crude oil amounting to 12.5 per cent of the posted price per barrel as a cost factor in calculating the taxable income of KOC. For that privilege, the oil companies were allowed to deduct from posted prices certain discounts they usually granted on their sales.

In addition to these payments to the government, there is another capital contribution from the oil sector to the private sector. This capital transfer represents the purchases of the oil companies from domestic suppliers, which includes wage and salary payments as well as purchases of equipment and materials from Kuwait. It also includes contract arrangements with Kuwaitis who carry out certain projects for the oil companies. All these payments have averaged about KD12 million a year. The dramatic increase in government oil revenue took place during the 1970s. This was the period when OPEC began to gain strength. As a result, posted prices rose several times. The Kuwaiti-government income per barrel increased from 82.5 cents before the 13 November 1970 to 94.6 cents during the last part of the year, and to 96.5 cents in early 1971. After the Tehran agreement the government income per barrel rose to $1.20 and then to $1.40. However, in December 1973 government income per barrel doubled to $2.80. Nevertheless, the really dramatic increase effectively took place in January 1974, when government revenue from the companies' equity became $6.9 and from the government's share of its sales rose to $10.73, as a result of the participation agreement. After the government took over KOC, the income per barrel accruing to the government increased to $11.50. From 1974 to the end of 1976 there were several small increases in the posted prices of crude oil as a result of OPEC's decision regarding compensation for inflation. During the 1973–5 period, oil production declined by 8.3 per cent in 1973, 15.7 per cent in 1974 and 18.15 per cent in 1975. That decrease in oil production did not bring about any decrease in government oil revenue: on the contrary, increased posted prices, higher royalties, partial participation and finally complete takeover of KOC by the government more than compensated for declining crude-oil exports. By 1974–5, oil revenue increased by more than 334 per cent but later declined by 15 per cent during 1976–7 as a result of reductions in oil exported.

2 (b) Capital transfer from the government to the economy: the growth of government expenditure

Table 3.4 shows the growth and gives a breakdown of government expenditure. Current expenditure has been increasing since 1952. As a percentage of the total govennment budget, and apart from other independent budgets, the increase was from 41.5 per cent in 1961-2 to 63.3 per cent for the period 1968-9. During the 1970s average annual expenditure reached as high as 75 per cent of the total budget. The main reasons for this increase were increasing government activity in all aspects of social, economic and political life and the increasing role of the government as an employer, absorbing the highest percentage of the labour force in Kuwait.

Capital expenditure on development covers almost every part of the infrastructure and has been increasing since 1952. With the exception of the period up to 1964, when land-purchase expenditure was greater, development expenditure surpassed all other expenditure, apart from current expenditure. If one breaks down investment in development according to various sectors, then the highest percentage for almost every year and up to 1965 is utilities, i.e. water and electricity. In 1964-5 about one-quarter of development investment was allocated to that sector alone. This reflects the critical need for water in a country where no rivers exist and where water has to be distilled from the sea. Also, with the growth of population and industry, electricity consumption increased and necessitated greater investment in power-generating plants. By 1977, however, this sector had been surpassed by the education and health services (see later).

A major source of government expenditure has been the land-purchase programme, begun in 1952. This was a by-product of the urbanization plan adopted by the Higher Council in 1952. The purchased land inside the old city of Kuwait was used for roads and public facilities. The unused part of the purchased land was re-sold to the private sector for commercial use. The price of land was artificially inflated, reaching as high as $700 per square foot. This was aggravated by the increasing dependence of the private sector on land purchase and speculation, rather than on capital investment.

From the macroeconomic point of view this kind of financial transaction by the private sector does not represent a net or gross addition to national income because both the government and the private sector buy an asset that is already in existence. The land-purchase philosophy had two main purposes. The first was to modernize Kuwait by demolishing the old houses in the old city of Kuwait. The government purchased these houses and lands at highly subsidized prices. At the same time the government sold new sites outside the city of Kuwait at lower prices to the displaced families, so that they could build new houses. The

Table 3.4 *Economic classification of government expenditure, 1961–75 (KD millions)*

Year	Current	% change	Development	% change	Transfers	% change	Land purchase	%
1961-2	67.12	41.5	35.67	22	0.81	0.5	58.86	36.0
1962-3	81.71	49.1	35.38	21.6	1.165	0.8	40.50	28.5
1963-4	99.44	50.6	50.35	26.5	3.2	1.7	32.0	21.6
1964-5	106.60	52.8	45.00	22.3	6.6	2.6	45.0	23.3
1965-6	122.8	55.0	57.60	25.8	15.6	6.1	29.20	13.1
1966-7	136.2	56.0	79.9	32.9	19.2	7.0	10.0	4.1
1967-8	154.9	52.2	62.7	21.8	44.7	15.6	30.0	10.4
1968-9	166.3	63.3	43.3	16.6	35.9	13.6	17.0	6.5
1969-70								
1970-1	230.9	66.54	47.9	13.80	43.8	12.62	24.4	7.03
1971-2	276.3	73.77	50.7	13.53	41.8	11.16	19.9	1.53
1972-3	313.3	74.33	60.2	14.30	24.1	5.88	23.2	5.50
1973-4	438.4	78.62	73.2	13.13	20.9	3.74	25.1	4.50
1974-5	821.5	74.28	128.7	11.64	20.7	1.87	135.0	12.21
1975-6	834.9	72.64	203.2	17.68	22.0	1.91	89.2	7.76
1976-7	792.0	72.12	203.0	18.48	23.1	2.1	80.0	7.28

Source: Ministry of Finance, Kuwait, 1977.

second purpose was to distribute part of the oil revenue to Kuwaiti citizens. Although no data are available on per capita distribution of the land-purchase programme. The wealthy families, who used to be engaged in sea trade and pearl-diving, possessed the largest houses inside the old city of Kuwait, and thus when the government started its land-purchase programme the owners of the vast lands and largest houses won the lion's share. The amount spent represented 24 per cent per annum of total government expenditure during 1960-5. Although the amount allocated to land-purchase programmes started to decline during the second half of 1960, it started to increase again by the beginning of 1970. However, the highest amount spent was during 1974-5, amounting to KD135 million.

The last item in the growth of government expenditure is social transfer, which covers the social-security system. In 1955 Kuwait began to enter the field of social security by giving financial aid to Kuwaiti families. Although this kind of financial help still exists, a new social-security fund has been established to deal with the problem at large. The amount spent annually far exceeds KD20 million. However, the most interesting part of the financial-aid policy is its coverage of a high percentage of the population in Kuwait. The number of Kuwaiti families benefiting from the financial-aid programme represents about 25 per cent of all the Kuwaiti families in the country. As to individuals, the beneficiaries represent around 17 per cent of the native population. These two percentages are the highest in the world. In most societies the former does not exceed 5 per cent. The increasing number of beneficiaries of financial aid has, however, created a feeling of dependence on the government. This feeling has been reinforced by the lack of serious vocational training.

Social-overhead capital

1 *Education*
The government has shown a keen interest in education, and expenditure has been increasing since the first oil exports from Kuwait in 1946. With the increase in the number of students and teachers, expenditure rose from KD8.82 million in 1960-1 to KD27.38 million in 1968-9. By 1977 it was in excess of KD100 million.

By virtue of its stage of development Kuwait had to recruit 90 per cent of its 163 teachers in 1946. The number increased to 5,615 in 1957. The annual increase in the number of teachers over a period of twenty years was 20 per cent. At the end of 1977 the number of teachers in government schools was more than 18,000.

This increase was made necessary by the increasing numbers of students attending schools in Kuwait. In 1946 there were 3,962 students including females. This number increased to 101,728 in 1966-7 and by the end of 1977 there were more than 250,000 students. In 1967 the government spent about $560 per student. (This subsidy included the non-Kuwaiti students also.) However, the cost of this subsidy increased due to the rise in the total number of students and the cost of living, and in 1977 it exceeded $600 per student. In addition, there were then about 3,000 students studying abroad, half of whom were on government scholarships. This figure is a relatively high one.

Despite the growth in the number of teachers and students and scholarships abroad, the educational system is unable to meet the local demands of every sector of the economy. The lack of comprehensive educational planning has resulted in a great financial loss to the Kuwaiti economy. It is also the case that the quality of the educational system in Kuwait, be it at primary-school level or at the university, has posed a problem: the lack of seriousness, discipline and clear objectives has jeopardized the future of the students and the country at large.

2 Health

Government expenditure on health has increased enormously. From a figure of KD5.9 million in 1957, it rose to KD15.72 million in 1968, culminating in a figure of KD60 million in 1977. This increase has been for a number of reasons. Kuwait provides a free health service to Kuwaitis and non-Kuwaitis alike and this had to cope with the rapid increase in population (mainly through large numbers of immigrants). Also, the government has placed more emphasis on curative rather than preventive medicine, the uncontrolled movement of the population making preventive medicine very difficult in practice.

Because of the increase in population and the availability of capital, the government increased the number of hospitals from two in 1949 to eleven in 1977. The Ministry of Health made remarkable efforts toward dispensions, dental clinics and school clinics. Equipping these health centres with medical staff increased the number of doctors from 45 in 1949 to more than 1,000 in 1977. Consequently the number of pharmacists, nurses, analysts, dentists, radiographers and health inspectors has increased over the past thirty years. The number of beds available for Kuwaitis and non-Kuwaitis has been increasing since the establishment of the first government hospital in 1949. (The hospital had 110 beds.) In 1977 the number of beds in hospitals increased to more than 4,000.

In spite of the availability of capital, Kuwait still ranks lower than some of the industrial countries in terms of number of beds per thousand of the population, or in terms of the number of doctors. The hospitals, though newly built, require a more efficient management and more effective maintenance programmes. Greater co-ordination between the Ministry of Health and the Ministry of Education would most surely lead to an increase in the present very low number of Kuwaiti doctors and qualified medical staff.

3 Housing

Since the early 1950s the government has been responsible for a series of housing programmes. This has been partly a response to the general development of Kuwait but is also a direct result of the state's commitment to the lower-income Kuwaitis[1] and to the Bedouins. As a result of this commitment, the lower-income Kuwaitis are given 25-year interest-free loans. In practice, repayment is often waived for reasons of poverty or death.[2]

The government is responsible for this housing programme through the Ministry of Public Works. It started with 14 houses in 1952 and reached an annual addition of about 500 houses between 1952 and 1967. During the past three years, however, the average number of houses reached a figure of about 1,500.

In addition to the houses built for the lower-income Kuwaitis by the Ministry of Public Works, there exists the Savings and Credit Bank, which has extended many loans to both limited- and unlimited-income Kuwaitis. The bank extends loans for building, buying and house maintenance, at very low rates of interest. Most loans have been for house construction, and they totalled more than KD20 million in 1976. Most of the loans went to married Kuwaitis who are above the lower-income group.

Despite the efforts made by the government, the problem of housing will remain for many years to come. Every year for the past thirty years the number of applications for low-income houses has increased while the ability to meet the demands of a large segment of the population has been handicapped by the administrative system. The justification for the capital surpluses enjoyed by the government cannot be based upon the allegation of limited absorptive capacity of the country. It is ironic that Kuwait, which enjoys the highest GNP per capita income suffers from this kind of problem. Apart from satisfying a basic human need, there is no doubt that improving living conditions improves health conditions and finally influences productivity — an important factor in economic growth.

The number of Kuwaiti and non-Kuwaiti families living in shacks is in excess of 14,000. Of that number, the proportion of Kuwaiti families far exceeds that of non-Kuwaiti families. This is the result of a naturalization policy that favours the Bedouins.

The question remains: What is the justification for this housing problem when there is available capital in the hands of the government? If the available data are correct then the problem must surely be one of general social policy and scientific planning. A further question is: How much money should be allocated by the government for the Kuwaitis living in shacks? The minimum cost per house built by the Savings and Credit Bank is said to have been KD3,084 in 1967. The present cost has increased this by a factor of ten for the same quality house built in the early 1960s. It totals about KD35,000 per house. Given the number of families in need of houses and given the cost of building, the total sum is only a minute percentage of total foreign deposits of surplus money in foreign banks. The more the government delays the solution of the housing problem the higher will be the cost both socially and financially. One might object that a cost-benefit analysis is needed instead of a naïve approach to the socio-economic problem. One can argue the primacy of economic efficiency, but with a lack of information and statistical data on general subjects the application of cost-benefit analysis will remain merely an academic exercise.

4 *Utilities*

(*a*) *Water* — Water is a rare commodity in Kuwait. There are no running rivers and the wells that exist are mainly brackish water; the geography is one of flat sandy plains. It is only natural, therefore, that successive governments should have given top priority to solving the water problem. Before the early 1950s Kuwait had depended on the brackish well water and on supplies of water brought in by boat from Iran. In 1953, however, the government commissioned the first distillation plant, producing sweet water. Production has increased enormously from 9 million gallons a day in 1967 to 13 million gallons in 1977. At the present time the total potable water from desalination plants and underground water is about 36.5 million gallons a day. The production of brackish water is about 24.5 million gallons a day. Total production is thus about 60 million gallons a day, or about 60 gallons per capita per day.

The cost of producing such water is still high, at more than $3 per thousand gallons. However, the water is sold at a price much lower than the cost of production.

Though there is a large number of houses connected to mains water supply, water is still sold at government water stations, from whence it is transported by private road tanker to be distributed to private houses.

The desalinated water is supplemented by supplies of sweet water from Salaibiya and Raudhatian wells. About 5 per cent of the water from the former is added to the distillate water to make it suitable for drinking. The balance of the water from these wells is used for irrigation and industry.

(b) *Electricity* — Investment in electric power has been increasing since 1951 and in 1964-5 more than KD10 million was invested in electricity and water. This figure increased to KD18.7 million in 1967-8 and by the end of 1977 the figure had more than doubled.

Before 1951 electric-power production did not exceed 30 megawatts and the number of consumers was less than eighty, almost all of them domestic users. However, the development of Kuwait has seen a massive increase. The growth in population and industry, together with the general government programme for urbanization, has led to more power stations to serve the increasing load. Power generated increased from 30 megawatts in 1951 to 1,364 megawatts in 1977.

The number of consumers increased from 5,067 in 1952 to 32,280 in 1958. With the influx of immigrants and the natural increase in population, the number of consumers reached its highest level in 1977, totalling more than 200,000. This has required more investment in electric utilities. An attendant problem to this increased consumption has been the consumption peak reached in summer: temperatures exceed 47 °C and people use refrigerators and air conditioners more. This heavy load usually reduces the voltage of the electric supply and power failures result. Legislation regulating voltage could prevent this.

The low price of electricity has meant extravagance on a large scale. Previously the rate was 13 fils per kilowatt-hour for both industrial and domestic use. That rate was first reduced to 4 fils and 6 fils per kilowatt-hour for industrial and domestic use respectively. Later on, the domestic charge was reduced further, to 2.5 fils per kilowatt-hour. This price reduction has undoubtedly encouraged an increase in electricity consumption, to the extent that some people leave their central air-conditioning on even if they are on holiday outside Kuwait. The main reason is to prevent the wallpaper from peeling off during the heat of summer. A further extravagance is the increasing trend to illuminate the walls surrounding the house at nighttime: the illumination is kept on all night. Unfortunately legislation has not been forthcoming to regulate this.

5 *Transport and communication*

Before the beginning of oil exports investment in transport and communication was meagre. The only major means of transport communication with the outside world was through the commercial fleet, which was mainly responsible for the growth of trade with India, East Africa, Iraq and Iran. Roads were unpaved and suitable only for transport by animal. Air transport was virtually non-existent. Telephones were limited to a few individuals and until 1956 the telephone system had less than 2,000 lines. The postal system was similarly limited. Now, however, all this is history.

With the growth of investment in social-overhead capital, more money was allocated to transport and communication. In 1964–5 about KD5 million was invested in that sector alone. This was increased to 7.5 million in 1966 and by the end of 1976 it was in excess of KD37 million. When the government started its urbanization plan there was hardly a paved road in all Kuwait (except the one connecting Kuwait city with Ahmadi, built by KOC in conjunction with its oil operators). By 1957, however, Kuwait had about 568 paved square kilometres. In 1958 there was an addition of 1,018 paved square kilometres and by the end of 1977 the area of paved roads was over 10,000 square kilometres. The number of cars using these roads increased from 30,000 in 1960 to more than 350,000 in 1977.

The development of sea and air ports was a result of the growth in imports and travel. The urbanization of Kuwait city and the plans made for new residential areas, together with the massive amount of money which went to the people through the land-purchase programme, accelerated the growth in imports and travel. Al-Mina was the only port handling dry cargo inside the city of Kuwait and it became unable to cope with the annually increasing tonnage. (This is apart from Mina Al-Ahmadi, which was established by KOC, and Mina Abdula, established by Aminoil, for the export of oil.) As a consequence the government built one of the largest sea ports in the Middle East, at Shuaikh. This port has a deep-water quay capable of unloading at any one time several ships exceeding 600 feet in length. In 1977 the number of ships unloading at Shuaikh was in excess of 1,800 and the tonnage exceeded 4.5 million metric tonnes of dry cargo. It is interesting to note that during the import boom of 1974, 1975 and 1976, the port of Shuaikh served the neighbouring countries as well, due to their congested ports. Dry cargo, after it was unloaded in Kuwait, was moved by land to Iraq, Saudi Arabia and the rest of the Arabian Gulf states.

The airport still remains in a very bad condition despite the availability of surplus capital. The government planned a long time ago to establish an international airport instead of the old airport but its plans never materialized. There were several reasons for this, among which was the lack of an overseeing body entrusted with the authority to ensure that the government's plans were fulfilled. (While this book was going to press a new airport was opened.)

There is only one Kuwaiti airline, Kuwait Airways, and that is owned by the government. The independent budget of the airline has increased with the years. It was about KD14.6 million in 1972 but reached more than 23 million in 1976. However, despite the monopoly position it enjoys in Kuwait it has been running at a loss since it was first established in 1954.

6 Shuaiba Industrial Development Board

The commission and duties of the Shuaiba Industrial Development Board were set out in the Amiri Decree of 14 May 1964 and could be summarized as follows:

> To construct, operate and maintain to the highest standards of industrial efficiency, an industrial estate capable of supplying resident industrial establishments with all supporting services required for the successful development of such industrial establishments.
>
> To conduct an active programme for the attraction of international and domestic investors.
>
> To promote and encourage the growth of heavy and medium industries for the diversification of the economy.
>
> To co-ordinate development of these industries with the overall economic development plans of the government.

To carry out its responsibilities towards the community and its industrial neighbours.

To apply accepted commercial principles and adopt industrial accounting methods in following this policy.

To conduct its operations in accordance with one-year, five-year, and longer templars concerning finance, personnel, operator services, facilities and industrial development.

To ensure that investors' plans are accommodated.

To achieve financial self-sufficiency within its combined operations over a ten-year period by operating on a breakdown basis of supervision for expansion and investment recovery.

To provide sufficient supporting services at the minimum cost needed to facilitate additional development (emphasis will be on efficiency, reliability, and economy of operation).

To conduct its activities with a maximum degree of decentralization by delegating appropriate authority to managers responsible for the port, utility services, industrial sites and other services and such functions as administration and finance.

To employ, train and develop Kuwaiti personnel whenever possible, and to promote its personnel on the basis of merit.

The total area of the Shuaiba industrial complex is about 8 square kilometres. It is provided with a modern harbour capable of handling more than a million tons per year of imports and exports. It also contains power stations in addition to a desalination plant with a capacity of more than 10 million gallons a day. The localized and integrated nature of these services makes their cost relatively cheap in addition to being supplied at highly subsidized prices. Unfortunately Shuaiba industrial area did not attract foreign investment because of the rigid commercial laws in Kuwait concerning foreign investment together with charging higher prices for gas as a feedstock to the petrochemical industry. Nevertheless, Kuwait National Petroleum Company and the Petrochemical Industries Company have benefited from the outside battery limit facilities. Despite that help, however, they were losing money every year up to 1974, when prices of oil and gas more than tripled.

The Shuaiba industrial area is still not self-sufficient: its expenditure still exceeds by far its revenue. In 1976–7 its expenditure exceeded KD11 million, while its revenue did not exceed KD4.6 million. In the field of training, there are still no qualified welders, joiners or plumbers.

In the field of community relations there is a deal of social tension because of the old problem of favour among friends and relatives. Finally, as far as management is concerned it is still centralized by the Ministry of Finance, with the ensuing bureaucratic dampers.

Nevertheless it must be said that Kuwait has benefited by building this kind of infrastructure long before any other Middle East country in general and the other Gulf states in particular. It has meant that foreign or domestic investment will be able to achieve a higher rate of return or lower costs than the other states. The reasons are first, the cost of construction was cheaper than it would be for any other state attempting to build a similar complex today (such as Saudi Arabia with Jubail). Second, all services are localized and integrated and relatively close to available labour. In other words, the social-overhead capital and the outside battery limits of the petrochemical industries are available and cheap.

7 The Savings and Credit Bank

The commercial banks in Kuwait are very conservative and are mainly concerned with two objectives: accumulation of domestic savings for outside short-term investment, and the financing of imports (which is very profitable). Kuwait is experiencing a commercial boom and a great capital surplus and the banks are happy with the situation. However, because of the nature of the commercial banks in Kuwait the government felt it necessary to establish the credit bank in October 1960. The bank set itself four objectives. First, it advances real-estate loans to Kuwaitis for building, repairing, extending or modernizing private dwelling places. Second, the bank offers real-estate secured loans, or loans guaranteed by the immobile assets of factories, to industrialists for founding, expanding or improving factories. Third, the bank advances loans to farmers for buying seed, fertilizer and agricultural equipment; for the installation of water pipelines; for drilling water wells in places where experts believe there to be subterranean water available. Fourthly, the bank gives loans to officials and government employees governed by Civil Service regulations and to members of the army and the armed forces governed by Law No. 27 for the year 1961, on security of salaries, gratuities, and pensions to which they may be entitled in accordance with the laws in force.

In July 1965, however, another important objective was added to the aims of the bank: the encouragement of savings. For this reason the name of the bank was changed to the Savings and Credit Bank, and its capital was increased from KD7.5 million to KD25 million, to be paid up from the general reserves of the state. The bank has no right to issue bonds but has the right to obtain loans from the government or, under its guarantee, sums which must not exceed twice its paid-up capital.

(*a*) *Management* – The management of the Savings and Credit Bank is controlled by a board of directors composed of the following members: a director-general as chairman; a deputy director as vice-chairman; three members who respectively represent the Ministry of Finance, the Ministry of Social Affairs and Labour, and the Ministry of Planning; six other members carrying on economic and financial business, appointed by the Minister of Finance for a renewable term of three years. The powers of the board of directors are very broad:

It discusses and approves the draft budget of the new fiscal year.

It approves contracts and agreements concluded by the bank.

It fixes the rate of interest, commission, and charges for other services provided by the bank.

It fixes the amortization rate of the bank's assets.

It decides whether to write off bad debts and make allowances for doubtful debts.

It settles the bank's claim by reconciliation and concludes arbitration agreements.

It sets up committees and prescribes the functions of such committees.

It promotes thrift by laying down plans which shall ensure the spread of thrift-mindedness among the public and various organizations.

It prescribes different kinds of savings accounts and fixes minimum and maximum balances for such accounts.

It lays down a policy for the investment of the bank's funds in the most lucrative way.

It determines, subject to the general economic policy of the state, the amount of return payable to savers.

It decides whether to open branches or agencies in Kuwait and whether to appoint agents and correspondents abroad.

It discusses and approves the establishment of new organs, the entering into partnerships with other similar bodies and the appropriation of other institutions.

Despite all these powers vested in the board of directors, however, the decisions of the board require the approval of the Minister of Finance; in fact, the Minister of Finance has the power of veto over all loans and all decisions taken by the board of directors, which puts the board in an advisory position rather than in a policy-making position. The chairman of the board is the managing director, which means that he is engaged in day-to-day operations besides his role as head of the board of directors. There is no specialization of roles, usually associated with a successful bank, especially if the bank has a broad field of operations, including real-estate credit, agricultural credit, industrial credit, and social credit, in addition to its role as a savings bank.

(b) *Activities of the bank* – The activities of the Savings and Credit Bank are reflected in its balance sheet. Loans are mainly concentrated in the real-estate field. In 1967 real-estate credit constituted fifteen times more in value than industrial, agricultural or social credit. In 1968 real-estate credit reached a value twenty times higher than any other credit, while in 1969 it jumped to twenty-two times more. During 1970-1 social credit reached 30.9 per cent of total loans and only 3 per cent went to industry; the balance was mainly in real estate. By the end of 1973 all industrial loans were terminated and became the major activity of the Industrial Bank of Kuwait. By the end of 1977 agricultural loans did not exceed 1 per cent of the total loans extended by the bank, while real-estate loans amounted to 94 per cent.

Prosperity and the very low interest rates charged by the bank facilitates the interest of the majority of borrowers in building houses and villas. (This does not include the lower-income groups.) Indeed, a very large number of Kuwaitis have been doing very good business building and selling houses. Agricultural loans, however, are limited by the high value of the land in relation to the agricultural product that might be produced. Almost all agricultural products are imported, since this is cheaper than producing them domestically. It is also true that water and the area of fertile land are very limited. For these reasons agricultural loans are small compared to real-estate loans.

Market contribution

1 Foreign trade

The statistical data of the balance of payments of Kuwait, although not quite accurate, do nevertheless reflect the nature of the

Kuwaiti economy. There are four main characteristics that stand out:

(1) The dependence of the whole economy on the export of one item, namely crude oil.
(2) The complete dependence on imports financed by oil revenue received by the government and its expenditure in the private sector.
(3) The high ratio of Kuwaiti foreign investment to domestic savings.
(4) The amount of current private transfer other than oil-company transfers.

The first characteristic has already been discussed in showing the contribution of the oil sector to the GNP. The second feature is a true reflection of the availability of a high-value single resource together with the absence of other natural resources. The third characteristic demonstrates the capital-surplus nature of the Kuwaiti economy and the growth of aid and foreign investment, whilst finally, the last characteristic is a reflection of the dependence of the economy on foreign labour.

(a) Imports

Kuwait has probably the highest per capita imports in the world. In 1968 it amounted to KD312, or about US $874, but by 1977 it had surged to KD693, or about US $2,460. This was mainly the result of the high-level of per capita income coupled with the absence of domestic manufacturing industries and agriculture.

Kuwait imports almost all of its needs except crude oil. The largest category of import is machinery and transport equipment, which amounted to 45.6 per cent of total imports in 1977. In the same year other manufactured goods, mainly comprised of household items, represented about 31 per cent of total imports. The third largest category of imports is food, which stands at almost 16 per cent. The next largest category − chemicals − might seem surprising for a country that possesses about all the raw material necessary for a chemical industry: the problem is that Kuwait suffers from a shortage of skilled manpower and technology to maintain a viable chemical industry, and there is a need to look at its general economic policy with a view to seeing how best this can be put right.

The western world is the main source of imports. The EEC provides the highest percentage of imports, at 33.8 per cent for 1977. The USA provides about 18 per cent of total imports, followed by Japan with 16 per cent. Kuwait's foreign trade with the communist countries is increasing at a steady rate, mainly with the People's Republic of China, Czechoslovakia, Romania, Hungary, Poland, Yugoslavia and the Soviet Union. China exports more to Kuwait than any other single communist country. Its share of Kuwait's imports stood at around 2 per cent in 1977. However, it must be stated that trade statistics with the communist countries underestimate the value of imports from the east European communist countries because importers (usually in Lebanon) change the name of the original source and put on a west European (or Lebanese) name. Apart from the communist countries, Kuwait's imports from the underdeveloped countries have been increasing since 1966, from 10 per cent of the total imports to around 13 per cent in 1977.

(b) Non-oil exports and re-exports

Exports other than oil have been increasing since 1963. During that year the value of non-oil exports did not exceed KD11 million. In 1968 their value doubled to KD22 million and later on increased to KD171 million.

Apart from fertilizer and shrimps, non-oil exports are re-exports to neighbouring countries. Saudi Arabia and the shaikhdoms of the Arabian Gulf import the highest portion of Kuwaiti re-exports. Iran is another market for re-export, effected by the Iranian labour force within Kuwait. As the Iranian workers go back home, they take with them large numbers of goods, varying from cloth to refrigerators. Some, in fact, buy the goods specifically to sell them in Iran, where they can make a good profit on them. These exports amounted to more than KD13 million in 1977.

Kuwait exports shrimps to the USA, the UK and to other western countries. It also exports fertilizer to several Asian states such as India and China and to many African states of the western and eastern shores of the continent. However, official trade statistics do not reflect the real value of exports and re-exports, for a number of reasons. First, fertilizer is sold at discounts that vary from time to time and from country to country depending on the supply and demand conditions of the world market for fertilizer and on how the political stance of the buyer is perceived. Second, shrimps are often shipped directly from outside Kuwaiti territorial waters, in which case it is not recorded in official statistical records. Third, re-exports are smuggled into the neighbouring countries and therefore are not, of course, recorded in the official statistical data.

(c) Private remittances

Private remittances reflect the dominance of the non-Kuwaiti element in the labour force, the majority of which is single males. These remittances are mostly directed to neighbouring countries such as Iraq and Iran. However, they go even further to Egypt, Syria, Yemen (North and South), Jordan and occupied Palestine. The private remittances to India and Pakistan are quite large and recently there has been an increase in the private remittances to European countries. This increase corresponds to the increase in non-Kuwaitis in the labour force. In 1965 the labour force was 184,297 and the foreign element stood at about 77 per cent of that figure; private remittances were more than KD60 million. However, by 1970 the labour force had risen to 242,197 and the foreign element had risen to 82 per cent; private remittances had increased accordingly to more than KD130 million. This increase in the foreign labour force continued and with it the private remittances more than doubled. In spite of this there is reason to believe that the value of private remittances has been underestimated, for the majority of private remittances to Iraq, Iran, Saudi Arabia and the Arabian Gulf shaikhdoms is cash transactions through friends or by the workers themselves who occasionally visit their countries. Also, Egyptian pounds can be bought at a very low price on the Kuwaiti capital market and then smuggled into Egypt.

2 The development of private and semi-private joint-stock companies

Table 3.5 shows the development of private and semi-private joint-stock companies. These companies are the result of the growth in wealth emanating from the oil industry and are part of increased government expenditure on social and economic development together with government capital transfer to the private sector through land-purchase programmes. Before 1950 there were no joint-stock companies at all; by 1968 the total value of such companies amounted to KD91 million. By the end of 1977 the authorized capital of Kuwaiti shareholding companies stood at more than KD346 million.

Table 3.5 *The development of private and semi-private Kuwaiti share-holding companies, 1977*

Name of Company	Date of establishment	Authorized capital (KD million)	Government participation (%)
National Bank of Kuwait	29.5.52	13,612,500	
Kuwait Cinema Company	5.10.54	1,635,263	Unknown
Kuwait Oil Tankers Co.	19.9.57	25,936,605	49
Commercial Bank	15.6.60	13,440,000	
Kuwait Insurance Co.	10.8.60	2,333,325	
Gulf Bank	29.10.60	7,044,465	
National Industries Co.	8.12.60	6,300,000	51
Kuwait Flour Mills Co.	25.10.61	2,000,000	50
Kuwait Investment Co.	3.12.61	11,269,130	50
Gulf Insurance Co.	7.4.62	2,560,000	Unknown
Al-Ahziya Insurance Co.	30.4.62	1,690,000	
Kuwait Hotels Co.	25.6.62	2,941,180	49
Kuwait Transport Co.	15.9.62	4,000,000	50
Kuwait Foodstuffs Co.	23.11.63	1,320,000	
Kuwait Foreign Trading & Contracting Co.	26.12.64	25,000,000	80
Metal Pipe Industries Co.	19.6.66	4,800,000	Unknown
Al-Ahli Bank	17.6.67	7,000,000	
Kuwait Cement Co.	23.10.68	6,500,000	28
Bank of Kuwait and the Middle East	27.11.71	8,000,000	49
Kuwait United Fisheries Co.	18.1.71	10,000,000	48
Kuwait Real Estate Co.	9.5.72	10,000,000	
Refrigeration and Cold Storage	15.2.73	4,000,000	25
United Real Estate	22.3.73	15,000,000	
Real Estate Bank of Kuwait	6.5.73	7,558,680	Unknown
National Real Estate Co.	24.6.73	12,600,000	70
National Automotive Manuf. & Trading Co.	10.7.73	3,600,000	
Kuwait International Investment	13.9.73	12.030,000	Unknown
Livestock Transport and Trade	24.11.73	9,968,176	
Shipbuilding and Repair Co.	30.3.74	10,000,000	Unknown
Kuwait United Poultry Co.	30.11.74	4,000,000	
Gulf Cables Co.	15.3.75	3,000,000	30
Sanitary Ware Industries	21.5.75	6,750,000	25
Burgan Bank	24.12.75	10,000,000	51
Melamine Industries	25.4.76	4,000,000	
Agricultural Food Products	26.5.76	10,000,000	
United Arab Navigation Co.	1.7.76	34,800,000	51
Warbah Insurance Co.	24.10.76	4,000,000	51
Kuwait Tyre Co.	28.11.76	8,000,000	
Kuwait Finance House	23.3.77	10,000,000	49
Overland Transport Co.	6.7.77	10,000,000	
		346,689,324	

Source: Ministry of Commerce and Industry, Kuwait, 1978.

71

With the growth of the private and semi-private joint-stock companies, the spirit of investment among Kuwaitis began to grow gradually. In 1952 the number of shareholders was 118 but this began to increase with the emergence of new companies. This fact surely reflects a change in attitude to money: it is no longer for consumption alone, neither is it for hoarding. This change in attitude has, however, been accompanied by strong speculative tendencies due to the nature of the Kuwaiti economy.

There is a tendency in the joint-stock companies for the shares to become concentrated in a few hands, especially with the commercial banks, insurance and investment companies. For example, the number of shareholders of the Gulf Bank at its date of incorporation in 1960 was 2,865. However, the number declined to 1,051 in 1967 and by 1977 the number of shareholders was not more than a few hundred. Again, the Kuwaiti Commercial Bank was subscribed to by 1,151 shareholders in 1960 but this number declined to 720 in 1967 and had declined even further by 1977. This tendency applies to almost all the banks and investment companies but is most striking amongst insurance companies. Industrial companies also show the same tendency but to a lesser degree.

The government is the prime mover of the economy. It is the largest employer and buyer of domestic products and services. Its role has increased during the past twenty years through its participation with the private sector in the development of joint-stock companies. This increasing role of the government was perceived by some observers of the Kuwaiti economy to reflect and augment the levelling-off of the construction boom and the decrease in allocation of money for land-purchase programmes in the 1960s. However, the construction boom continued and the increasing role of government participation in the development of joint-stock companies became wider and more penetrating and at the same time the money allocated for land-purchase programmes more than doubled. The government has two main objectives in creating joint-stock companies. First, is to diversify the economy in order to lessen the degree of dependence on the oil sector. Second, is to create a business atmosphere in order to attract young Kuwaitis to enter the market rather than join the government, which is already overstaffed. As a result, a large number of excellent employees has left the government and joined the private or semi-private sector with the end result backfiring against the government.

The range of government participation in joint-stock companies varies from one company to another and from one sector to another. The lowest rate of government participation is about 25 per cent, while the maximum participation is more than 80 per cent. The number of companies in which the government has a certain percentage participation is more than twenty. This is a very striking tendency, especially in a small stock market in which the total number of trading companies is only forty. Government participation covers almost every sector of the economy. It participates in industrial companies, transport, banking, insurance, investment, real estate and other services companies.

The Industrial Bank of Kuwait

The Industrial Bank of Kuwait was established during the latter part of 1973. Its formation was the result of government dissatisfaction with the policy of the commercial banks towards industry in Kuwait. At the request of the government the bank was established with the private sector with share capital of KD10 million. Table 3.6 lists shareholders corresponding with the equity holding.

Table 3.6

Government of Kuwait	3,500,000
Central Bank of Kuwait	1,400,000
National Bank of Kuwait	1,000,000
Commercial Bank of Kuwait	500,000
Gulf Bank	500,000
Al-Ahli Bank of Kuwait	500,000
Bank of Kuwait and the Middle East	500,000
Kuwait Flour Mills Company	500,000
Kuwait Metal Pipe Industries Co.	500,000
Kuwait National Industries Co.	500,000
Real Estate Bank of Kuwait	300,000
Kuwait Re-Insurance Co.	75,000
Kuwait Insurance Co.	75,000
Gulf Insurance Co.	75,000
Ahlia Insurance Co.	75,000
TOTAL	**10,000,000**

The objectives of the bank are sixfold. First, is to develop a long-term strategy for the industrial growth of Kuwait. In fact, this first objective is entrusted to the Ministry of Planning and therefore it remains as a doublification of objectives and efforts. The second objective of the bank is to initiate industrial projects and investment in the most promising sectors; most of the projects so far financed, however, have come at the initiative of Kuwaiti businessmen. The third objective of the bank is to provide equity and medium- and long-term credits for new, sound and viable projects. Since the formation of the Industrial Bank the financing of new projects has been on the increase and the bank has financed more than eighty-five projects worth around KD135 million. The bank has provided these projects with finance totalling about KD63.8 million. The largest share of the financing – some 70 per cent – was allocated to projects involving construction materials, metal products and engineering. Such products represent 60 per cent of the total number financed.

The fourth objective of the bank is to provide financing outside Kuwait to the extent that this benefits Kuwaiti industry and its development. This is a very important objective but unfortunately only two projects have been financed. The first involved the quarrying, crushing and shipping of aggregates from Ras Al-Khaimah to Kuwait; the second a study of the feasibility of manufacturing some of the desalination units at the Arab shipbuilding-and-repair yard in Bahrain.

It is much more important for the bank to find suitable projects outside Kuwait but in which some of the raw material can be produced in Kuwait (such as low-density polyethylene, ethylene glycol and styrene) and then shipped to countries where labour costs are low and the market large. An example is the textile industry, where the raw materials could be shipped from Kuwait to Morocco and then large plants could be established to use the low-cost labour to produce goods for domestic consumption for the American and European markets. Similarly, certain petrochemical raw materials could be produced in Kuwait and then several intermediate and final products could be produced in joint ventures with companies well established in their fields and with large capital shares in the market. Such a policy would assure Kuwait the sales of its product and would give it access to marketing and technical know-how through on-the-spot training of its labour and management.

The fifth objective of the bank is the transfer of technology to Kuwait and the development of domestic money and capital markets. The former was to be effected by Kuwaiti businessmen in joint venture with foreign companies, or through buying the rights to use their technology. However, to date the bank has yet to be effective in this area. Although the bank did not stress in its charter the importance of the development of the domestic money and capital markets as a primary objective, nevertheless its efforts in this field have been quite successful. In joint venture with Kuwait International Investment Company, the Industrial Bank formed a new company in April 1977 named the Arab Company for Trading Securities. The aim of this company was to maintain a secondary market in Kuwaiti dinar denominated bond issues, certificates of deposit and Eurocurrency bond issues involving Arab management or underwriting. Both the bond issues and the certificates of deposit were well received because they provided the individual investors and corporate treasurers with better results. However, the latter helped to destroy the rigidity in choosing between KD fixed deposits and KD bonds. The bank was also instrumental in assisting the development and the growth of medium-term loans expressed in KD and other currencies at fixed and floating rates.

The Industrial Bank of Kuwait has played an important role since its formation in 1973. However, through improvement of its management, and close co-operation and co-ordination with the Ministries of Finance, Oil, and Social Affairs and Labour, Kuwait could build a better industrial sector both inside and outside Kuwait. The bank should not only finance the import of equipment and its installation but also the training of the labour force, which is its most valuable asset. In its co-operation with the Ministry of Finance and the Central Bank most of the speculative commercial activities characterizing the Kuwaiti stock exchange could be reduced and therefore more savings could be channelled into productive investment activities.

Foreign aid

Kuwait entered the field of foreign aid early in its economic development. It has extended this aid to others through three main channels: the Kuwaiti Fund for Arab Economic Development (KFAED); the General Authority for South Arabic and Arabian Gulf States; and state reserves and the government budget.

General Authority for South Arabic and Arabian Gulf States
This authority began in 1962 under the title Gulf Permanent Assistance Committee (GUPAC) and was intended to provide grants to the Gulf Trucial States, mainly for social projects such as health and education. General surveys are also made freely available to national and foreign investors to determine the development potential of the area. The General Authority considers its disbursements as outright grants.

GUPAC was responsible for the running of more than thirty-two schools, two hospitals and more than seven out-patient clinics. It also financed the building of two sanitoriums and more than four hospitals, twelve schools and fifty houses for personnel.

The Gulf Committee became interested in the Yemen after the coup that ousted the Imam, and it financed the construction of more than twenty schools and teachers' colleges and seven clinics. The interest of the committee was also intensified after the unification and independence of South Yemen.

Kuwaiti Fund for Arab Economic Development

The Kuwaiti Fund for Arab Economic Development is the largest financial institution for the financing of economic projects in the Arab and less-developed countries. It was established in December 1961 with a capital of KD50 million. In 1963 this capital was raised to KD100 million. After the high rate of increase in crude-oil prices its capital became KD1 billion in 1974. Unlike the General Authority for South Arabic and Arabian Gulf States, the fund's main purpose is to give loans for purely economic projects — it does not finance projects of a medical or social nature.

In general, KFAED follows strict business practice. Before undertaking any project, it has to assess its economic priorities, technical feasibility and its financial soundness. Unfortunately, the fund does not attempt to calculate its contribution to the GNP of the countries in which it is investing. The interest rate charged by the fund ranges from 2.5 per cent to 3.5 per cent, plus 0.5 per cent service charge. The fund is also generous in financing feasibility studies and in accepting maturities ranging from twelve to twenty-five years. The fund also hopes to raise its standard in the international capital markets to be able to combine Arab and foreign capital for the development of the less-developed countries.

The fund is run by a board of directors under the chairmanship of the Minister of Finance. These eight members are responsible for the decision-making of the fund. However, the influence of the Prime Minister and the Minister of Foreign Affairs may well be decisive.

As with all foreign-aid programmes the motives behind Kuwait's foreign-aid programme are a mixture of ethics, economics, and politics, whether the aid comes from KFAED or from state resources. However, where aid is from state resources political motives are, by the very nature of the aid, generally more prominent.

Financial record
The financial aid given by Kuwait to the less-developed countries, be they Arab or non-Arab countries, is a real transfer of wealth emanating from a non-renewable source of income. This is the major difference between the aid programmes of Kuwait and the western industrial or communist countries. The aid burden on Kuwait is heavier than, for example, the USA or Great Britain, because Kuwait gives its aid as part of its capital. This is being realized through several institutions, such as KFAED; the Arab Fund for Social and Economic Development; the OPEC special fund; the Arab Bank for Economic Development in Africa; the World Bank; and, finally, the International Monetary Fund. Through all these institutions several millions of dollars were transferred from Kuwait to the less-developed countries. The total net flows are shown in Table 3.7.

Table 3.7

	1973	1974	1975	1976
Amount ($ millions)	550.0	1,250.1	1,711.2	1,874.8
As % of GNP	9.17	11.46	11.44	11.50

The financial record is impressive. The total net flow has increased from $550 million in 1973 to more than $1,874 million in 1976. As a percentage of GNP it has increased from 9.17 per cent to 11.50 per cent during the same period. This is strikingly significant, especially if it is known that this total net inflow of capital emanates from the oil sector, which itself represents more than 75 per cent of GNP.

Future policy for KFAED
The Kuwait Fund is still regarded by Kuwaitis and foreigners as a political entity rather than as a pure financial institution with future economic benefits for Kuwait. This view stems particularly from a large segment of the merchant class in Kuwait and the lower-income groups which are suffering from a high rate of inflation and lower real income. Further criticism of the fund has arisen because of the mystery surrounding its activities, which in turn stems from the lack of specialized departments with specific responsibilities. The critics would like to see the heads of the present departments demonstrating more autonomy in initiating new projects and ideas.

In a real world there is no such thing as an ideal institution, be it financial or otherwise. The Kuwait Fund developed initially as a response to a political need. Now that it has achieved its political goal, or let us believe that it did, other goals and objectives should be created, so that the Kuwait Fund is cherished by both the average man in Kuwait and the government. Advisers have suggested to the top policy-makers in Kuwait that the following objectives should, in the near future, be priority goals for the Kuwait Fund.

First, the fund should contribute to the economic benefits of the labour force in Kuwait. At the present time there is no such contribution whatsoever. The fund, in employing consultants to study projects in the less-developed countries, always refers to outside consultants in all sorts of fields. This policy, if it is continued, will deprive a large number of Kuwaiti consulting firms from the potential benefits inherent in the participation in such projects. Although the government is trying to develop the services sector of the economy, it has not co-ordinated its strategy in the consulting field. In the coming years many Kuwaiti agro-economists, engineers, architects, etc., will be flooding into Kuwait both from universities inside and outside the state. Naturally, not all of them will join the bureaucracy of the government, and it is not desirable that they should do so. Perhaps it will be better for the Kuwait Fund to organize a huge consulting pool to make use of this expertise, working at first with well-established foreign consulting firms until they have learnt the practical side of the business. Later they could stand on their own, as a contributing sector to the GNP of Kuwait and the countries receiving aid.

Second, the Kuwait Fund should contribute to the development of the capital and money markets in Kuwait. It could do so by creating a secondary market in KD denominated bond issues and certificates of deposit. It could involve not only Kuwaiti capital in the development of the less-developed countries but also international capital could be mobilized under the direction of the Kuwait Fund for the benefits of the less-developed world. One instrument by which international capital could be mobilized for the development of the less-developed countries is the guaranteeing of loans extended by the international commercial banks. This means is stated in the charter of the Kuwait Fund but unfortunately it is rarely used.

Third, the Kuwait Fund gives soft loans only to government-controlled projects which lie mainly in the sphere of social-overhead capital, such as roads, power stations, irrigational projects. However, it is intended that in the near future the fund should be able to extend loans to projects within the private sector and mainly in those which lie in the field of direct agricultural and industrial activities. This future policy will enable Kuwait equity capital to participate in the development of the Arab countries enjoying ample natural resources and skilled labour. This policy is being pursued by the Industrial Bank of Kuwait at present but it would have been better to have implemented it in the first place.

Fourth, after the increase in the prices of crude oil, the activities of the Kuwait Fund were extended beyond the Arab countries and therefore included all the less-developed countries in Asia, Africa and South America. The policy has increased the financial commitment of the fund, which is mainly coming from a non-renewable resource. As compensation for its enlarged activities, the fund should follow a new policy. Any given loan should be divided into two parts. The large portion of the loan, say 80–90 per cent, should be extended as a soft loan, at the same terms followed as at the present time. The smallest portion of the loan, the remaining 10–20 per cent, should be extended to the recipient country, be it the private or government sector, at commercial terms. This portion of the loan could be given by the fund or investment companies and banks. The main purpose of this policy would be to protect Kuwait from the vagaries of foreign-currency fluctuation, depreciation and devaluation. At the same time it would encourage the Kuwaiti private sector and the government to increase their investment in the less-developed countries. This is not only desirable politically but is required economically by Kuwaiti capital.

Chapter 4

The dualistic nature of the economy

(a) Kuwaiti National Income Account

In response to the rapid economic development, the government of Kuwait has felt it necessary to have a clear picture of the various sectors of the national economy. This has arisen out of the conviction that an accurate national-income account is a necessity for sound economic planning and economic policies. To achieve this purpose, the government asked the International Bank for Reconstruction and Development (IBRD) to prepare a national-income account for Kuwait. The first attempt by the IBRD, in 1961, was to construct a national-income account for the year 1959, but due to the scanty information available on the various economic aspects of Kuwait the result was very much a rough estimate. The second IBRD mission, in 1962, tried again to measure national income, this time for the year 1962-3. Although there was more information available than with the first mission, there were still many obstacles and results were again far from precise.

With the establishment of the Kuwaiti Planning Board, and later on the Ministry of Planning with its various departments, more information became available on the economic sectors in Kuwait. The population censuses of 1970 and 1975 were more accurate and inclusive than the previous ones of 1957, 1961 and 1965. The Ministry of Planning, instead of relying on IBRD missions, began to call on various academic institutions, such as Stanford Research Centre. (Recently, however, the Ministry of Planning has had more faith in the ability of private companies to examine the economy and present an overall analysis of the national economy.) Nevertheless, in spite of the availability of more accurate information and the setting up, in theory, of a five-year plan, the government did not seem eager to implement the plans or even to use some of the financial or monetary tools to direct the economy towards a national economic plan.

The first part of this chapter will show the rate of growth of the GNP from 1962 to 1977. A clearer picture of the economy will then be presented by a sectoral distribution of GDP. The whole aggregate of the GDP will be divided into two larger sectors: the oil sector and the non-oil sector. This method of sectoral distribution will reveal more accurately the nature of the Kuwaiti economy but it will also show the composition of the labour force, where a special dualistic nature of manpower is revealed.

1 Rate of growth of GNP

Kuwait has developed rapidly over a short period of time. The annual growth rate for the GNP for the period 1962–3 to 1967–8 was 8.8 per cent. The major factors contributing to this high rate of growth were the rapid development of the oil industry, increasing oil production and the phenomenal influx of immigrants. However, this 8.8 per cent rate of growth is very small when compared with the latter years, from 1967–8 to 1976–7. During this latter period the growth rate for the GNP averaged 12 per cent, mainly because of the increasing posted prices of crude oil and liquefied petroleum gas and increasing government expenditure and rising economic private activity. This period in the economic history of Kuwait witnessed the highest rate of registration of industrial companies, banks, investment companies, insurance companies and real-estate companies.

The GNP growth rates for different years are always proportional to the rates of oil export, oil prices and government expenditure. Table 4.1 shows that the growth rate for the GNP for the year 1965–6 was remarkably low compared with previous years. The increase was no more than 4.2 per cent. This was the result of the low rate of growth of the oil sector in that year and the decline in the percentage of government expenditure in the previous year 1964–5, during which less money was spent on development projects and land-purchase programmes. Conversely, the growth rate for the GNP for the year 1966–7 was remarkably high, approaching 13 per cent, the main contributing factors being the increase in the rate of growth of oil exports and increased government expenditure. However, during the period of spending 1970–7, the main factor leading to the higher (and unprecedented) rates of growth was higher oil prices, resulting in higher government revenues and higher government expenditure.

2 Per capita GNP

A proper study of income distribution in Kuwait is almost impossible because of the lack of accurate data on income and wealth. There is no personal income tax and, therefore, no financial and monetary record. Although there is corporate tax legislation, the companies working in Kuwait, whether in joint venture with foreign firms or purely Kuwaiti companies, pay neither any tax nor submit to the authorities concerned any financial record of substance. Capital-gains tax does not exist either, in spite of the high level of speculation on the Kuwaiti stock exchange and in real estate and land trading. Import duties are very low and the profit margins of the merchants are high. In addition, the value of imported goods is sometimes underestimated in order to reduce the already low import duties. Others do not pay import fees at all. The only companies that paid taxes are the oil companies, and now almost all of these are government owned.

Income and wealth are not evenly distributed in Kuwait. This is partly a matter of inherited wealth and position, which has allowed subsequent profitable investment in banking, insurance, industry and international concerns. It is also the case, however, that the land-purchase programme – intended to distribute the wealth among the Kuwaiti population – allowed a number of individuals, through foresight or foreknowledge, to become very wealthy. Land was bought comparatively cheaply and then sold, at great profit, to the government, who purchased the land for their various planning projects.

The large majority of the Kuwaiti population that is legally considered part of the labour force is government employees. Most of them belong to the lower-income group, which earns very low incomes by Kuwaiti standards. Since the non-Kuwaitis in the labour force exceed 75 per cent, and since they are not allowed to own buildings or dwellings, it goes without saying that a large percentage of them represent the lowest income group in Kuwait, especially because the largest portion of their income is spent on rent. However, it must be said that some of the educated non-Kuwaitis with marginal skills have benefited considerably by managing and running Kuwaiti businesses in joint ventures with Kuwaiti businessmen; but that joint-venture process between Kuwaitis and non-Kuwaitis which directed some wealth to the latter does not apply to the large majority of skilled non-Kuwaitis such as doctors, teachers and engineers.

Although the concept of per capita GNP is meaningless as far as income and equality are concerned, its mention in the context of the Kuwaiti economy is relevant. During the period from 1962 to 1968, the per capita GNP of Kuwait was fluctuating, as shown in Table 4.1. The

Table 4.1 *Rate of growth of GNP and per capita GNP distribution, 1962-3 to 1976-7*

Year	GNP (KD million)	Rate of growth (%)	Population ('000)	Per capita GNP (KD)
1962-3	460	–	–	–
1963-4	500	8.6	–	1,008
1964-5	542	8.4	400	1,325
1965-6	565	4.2	480	1,177
1966-7	635	12.4	525	1,210
1967-8	692	9.0	610	1,134
1968-9	793	14.6	660	1,202
1969-70	840	5.9	720	1,167
1970-71	909	8.2	792	1,148
1971-2	1,151	26.6	870	1,323
1972-3	1,274	10.7	880	1,448
1973-4	1,859	45.9	890	2,089
1974-5	3,169	70.5	900	3,521
1975-6	3,503	10.5	1,000	3,503
1976-7	4,377	24.9	–	–

Sources: Kuwait Institute of Economic and Social Planning in the Middle East, Research Monograph No. 1, *National Accounts of Kuwait 1965/66 to 1967/9*; Ministry of Planning, Statistical Abstract 1977, Central Statistical Office of Kuwait; Ministry of Planning, Central Statistical Office of Kuwait, population censuses, 1965, 1970, 1975.

probable explanation for this is to be found in the difference between the rate of growth of the population and the rate of growth of GNP. The United Nations mission of 1961 estimated the GNP for 1959 at KD296 million (about $3,000 per capita). The second mission of 1963 estimated GNP at KD 370 million and per capita GNP fell to $2,960 in 1962-3. Both estimates of GNP were based on the exclusion of retained profits and foreign-exchange expenditure of the foreign oil companies. On the basis of the IBRD estimate, the per capita GNP declined by 7.5 per cent from 1959 to 1963. This rate of decline could be ascribed to the striking increase in population, which reduced the oil revenue per capita from about $1,600 in 1959 to less than $1,400 in 1963.

The per capita GNP reached its highest level in 1964-5 (for the period under study) and then declined. The interesting point to note is that in 1968 although GNP recorded a fairly high rate of growth (9 per cent), per capita GNP had fallen to KD1,134. Again the reasons are a higher rate of population growth and the low quality of the labour force and its percentage of the total population. However, in recent years, especially from 1970 to 1977, per capita GNP has been rising all the time due to the increase in oil and gas prices, to the extent that the increase in population during that period had no influence on the level of GNP per capita. In 1976-7 the per capita GNP was in excess of KD4,000 (or $14,000).

(b) The dualistic nature of GDP: oil versus non-oil sector

The gross domestic product accounts of Kuwait, when taken in their aggregate form, do not reflect the true nature of the economy. Although the use of the concept of GNP is inappropriate for reasons mentioned in chapter 3, nevertheless if one uses the method employed by the Planning Board and breaks down the GDP into oil and non-oil sectors, then there appears to be a sizeable exaggeration of the locally produced goods and services.

Table 4.2 shows the value of expenditure at constant market prices for the years 1965-6 and 1975-6. It is clear that the value of expenditure in the oil sector greatly surpasses that in the non-oil sector. It was 63.4 per cent of GDP for the year 1965-6 as compared with 36.6 per cent for the non-oil sector during the same year. As a result of increasing oil and gas prices, the oil-sector contribution to the GDP increased to 70 per cent in 1975-6, with the contribution of the non-oil sector decreasing to 30 per cent. The facts emphasize the dualistic nature of the economy; however, in reality it is even more dualistic in the sense of a heavy dependence on crude-oil exports.

Even if one breaks down the non-oil sector into its components, a pyramidic picture could be derived from a hierarchical dependence originating from government expenditure, which in itself depends on oil revenue. The wholesale and retail trade represents the highest percentage in terms of expenditure in the non-oil sector in 1965-6. It amounted to 8 per cent of GDP. It declined to 5.78 per cent in 1975-6 due to the contribution of the oil sector and more economic activity in the other sub-sectors of the non-oil sector, such as finance, public administration, defence, industry and real estate.

Table 4.2 *Distribution of GDP between the oil sector and the non-oil sector*

Sectors	1965-6 (%)	1975-6 (%)
The oil sector	63.4	70
The non-oil sector:	36.6	30
Public administration and defence	5.5	8.54
Wholesale and retail trade	8.0	5.78
Industry	3.2	4.9
Finance, insurance and real estate	0.8	4.6
Transport, storage and communication	2.8	2.58
Electricity, water and municipality services	2.1	2.35
Construction	4.3	0.9
Others		0.35

Sources: Ministry of Planning Statistical Abstract 1977, Kuwait, 1978; Central Bank of Kuwait, Economic Report for 1977, Kuwait, 1978.

1 Industry

The industrial sector made a greater contribution to GDP during the period 1966-74 than during previous years, despite the fact that the domestic market is small and other factors of production or other national resources are scarce. Table 4.3 clearly shows that the number of industrial establishments increased from 995 in 1966 to 1,549 in 1974 and the number of employees in those industrial establishments increased from 10,155 to 16,733 during the same period. The value of industrial production more than trebled. It jumped from KD24.5 million to KD84.1 million, and the value added surged from KD1.1 million to KD30.4 million. With the establishment of the Industrial Bank of Kuwait in 1973 more industrial establishments were built, covering the food, beverage, furniture and metal industries. The fairly cheap finance offered by the bank encouraged some Kuwaiti-businessmen towards industry, in spite of their traditional attachment to trade and real estate. This new attitude toward industry increased the value of industrial production to KD75 million in 1973-4.

It must be emphasized, however, that most industry in Kuwait, other than oil and gas, is based on simple processing and largely depends on imports of primary capital, materials and intermediate goods. The paint industry is wholly imported and what is done in Kuwait is the mixing operation. All kinds of metals are imported and then cut and welded to specific designs in Kuwait. The same applies to food and

85

Table 4.3 *Growth of the manufacturing sector, 1966–74*

Sub-sector	No. of Establishments			Employments			Value added (KD million)			Production (KD million)			Average annual rate of growth			
													Valued Added		Employments	
	1966	1971	1974	1966	1971	1974	1966	1971	1974	1966	1971	1974	1966–71	1971–4	1966–71	1971–4
Food and Beverages	397	443	462	3,375	4,137	4,499	3.7	4.0	4.5	8.8	15.5	24.2	0.02	0.04	0.05	0.3
Furniture	363	671	620	2,300	4,254	3,786	2.4	5.3	6.7	5.1	11.5	16.1	0.24	0.09	0.16	0.4
Paper and Printing	16	31	37	431	970	1,266	0.6	1.2	1.8	0.8	2.6	5.0	0.40	0.17	0.25	0.0
Chemical	4	8	11	327	1,169	1,551	0.2	1.5	5.2	0.7	6.1	12.5	1.30	0.82	0.51	0.1
Non-metals	116	131	148	2,629	3,180	3,308	3.0	3.6	6.6	6.5	8.7	14.4	0.04	0.28	0.04	0.1
Metals	99	246	271	1,093	2,214	1,323	1.2	2.7	5.6	2.6	5.2	12.9	0.25	0.36	0.20	0.2
TOTAL	995	1,530	1,549	10,155	15,924	16,733	1.1	19.5	30.4	24.5	49.6	84.1	0.15	0.19	0.11	0.2

Source: Central Statistical Office of Kuwait, Ministry of Planning, Annual Statistical Abstract 1977.

beverages — the main ingredients are imported but are mixed domestically. Almost all the materials involved in the building industry are imported from abroad, with the exception of sand and a small volume of aggregates. A large volume of domestic furniture is being produced in Kuwait but again often almost everything is imported, including the labour. The Kuwaiti added value lies in the cutting, nailing and polishing. Yet, because of the high level of income in Kuwait and the expensive locally produced furniture, most of the Kuwaiti population tend to favour fully imported furniture, which is relatively cheap and of better quality and design. It is especially cheap if it is imported direct by the user, because a high margin of profit is thereby eliminated.

2 Finance, insurance and real estate

The contribution of this sub-sector to the GDP was 0.8 per cent in 1965-6. By 1975-6, however, its contribution had increased to nearly 5 per cent. Over that period, more banks and investment companies were registered and came into operation. Newly established public-share real-estate companies became a novelty in the 1970s. The assets of the commercial banks increased from KD337 million in 1973 to KD2.4012 billion in 1977. The claims of the commercial banks on the private sector jumped from KD266.3 million in 1973 to KD1.2421 billion in 1977. Table 4.4 shows the distribution of the commercial banks' credit, by economic sector.

Table 4.4 *Commercial banks' credit, by economic sector (KD million)*

	1973	1974	1975	1976	1977
Trade	81.0	121.3	165.9	292.4	375.6
Industry	11.9	15.6	24.8	35.2	49.2
Construction	53.4	80.5	97.0	166.7	199.4
Agriculture and fisheries	12.8	9.1	9.9	14.3	20.0
Financial services	38.6	47.4	93.8	169.6	216.3
Personal loans	48.9	77.8	72.7	171.1	212.6
Total	246.6	351.7	464.1	849.3	1073.1

Source: Central Bank of Kuwait, Economic Report for 1977, Kuwait, 1978, p. 104.

Table 4.4 shows that the activities of the banks are most concentrated on trade and that is mainly import financing. Financial services consists mainly of personal loans for real-estate purchase and speculation and, more recently, personal loans for stock purchase. The latter has inflated the shares of the stock market in Kuwait and resulted in some personal wealth and some bankruptcies.

Before 1965 there were no real-estate companies or investment companies apart from the Kuwait Investment Company. By the end of 1977, however, the assets of the investment companies exceeded KD399 million. Over the past ten years many investment companies have been established, but only very few of them are public shareholding companies and the remainder are closed companies or family businesses.

The same applies to real-estate companies. Before 1965 there were no public shareholding real-estate companies, but by the end of 1977 there were more than 4 – that is, apart from other companies whose main objectives are not directed towards real estate, such as Kuwait Foreign Trading, Contracting and Investment Company. The main reasons for the entry of other companies into the real-estate field is the high profits realized in that sub-sector of the economy, and the speculative activities, supported unfortunately by government policy. However, one must say – without falling into the mistake of generalization – that most of the Kuwaitis who do not belong to the limited-income group derive their income apart from salaries and wages from rents, to the extent that the Kuwaiti economy should be classified as a rentier economy.

Finally, it should be noted that in analysing the components of the sub-sectors of the non-oil sector one is dependent on government statistics. These are sometimes overestimated and sometimes underestimated. Industry, for example, provided 3.2 per cent and 4.9 per cent of GDP in 1965 and 1975 respectively. However, these figures are overestimated, because in addition to the value of domestic production the value of imported goods is calculated in arriving at the value of domestically produced goods. It is also to be emphasized that details of individual and family financial and real-estate transactions are not readily accessible and therefore accurate accounts are difficult. It is mostly a matter of underestimation because of the lack of financial records. Suffice it to say that in the latter sub-sector it is finance and real estate that have been increasing over the past ten years. Most successful businessmen in Kuwait have been working in these two sub-sectors – an indication of their lucrative and high-volume activities.

(c) The dualistic nature of manpower

The second kind of dualism in the Kuwaiti economy is evidenced by the distribution of the employed population according to economic

Table 4.5 *Labour force by sex, nationality and division of economic activity in census years, 1957, 1965, 1970, 1975*

Sections of economic activity	Sex	Census 1975 non-Kuwaiti	Kuwaiti	Census 1970 non-Kuwaiti	Kuwaiti	Census 1965 non-Kuwaiti	Kuwaiti	Census 1957 non-Kuwaiti	Kuwaiti
Agriculture, hunting and fishing	M	3,522	3,970	3,253	798	1,408	666	446	603
	F	9	13	5	4	2	7	–	–
Mining and quarrying	M	2,953	1,767	4,828	1,627	5,241	1,337	4,088	1,211
	F	127	12	668	48	402	12	106	–
Manufacturing industries	M	21,889	2,237	25,876	6,100	16,103	1,823	5,539	1,009
	F	320	21	106	9	14	2	43	20
Construction	M	30,357	1,755	31,418	2,186	17,566	1,262	8,025	378
	F	143	1	66	2	18	2	–	–
Electricity, gas and water	M	5,230	2,029	5,106	2,130	5,341	1,645	–	–
	F	7	5	13	3	5	–	–	–
Wholesale and retail trade	M	32,364	6,297	25,181	7,261	17,769	5,115	4,058	4,107
	F	868	30	534	37	147	14	15	44
Transportation and communication	M	10,853	4,305	9,640	2,357	7,336	2,612	2,053	1,513
	F	265	262	136	5	76	1	–	–
Services	M	76,751	57,306	54,401	34,919	50,123	24,571	27,697	14,365
	F	25,786	6,959	12,909	1,907	6,892	948	1,522	316
Activities not adequately defined	M	–	–	559	236	611	232	3,583	4,803
	F	–	2	21	5	64	17	7	4
Total activity	M	183,919	79,666	160,262	57,614	131,498	39,163	55,489	27,989
	F	27,525	7,305	14,458	2,020	7,620	1,003	1,693	384
	T	211,444	86,971	174,720	59,634	139,118	40,166	57,182	28,373
Inactive	M	17,206	38,863	17,341	43,123	10,240	25,583	6,180	10,472
	F	86,634	112,812	68,938	96,894	35,580	60,772	10,430	34,903
Total population	M	201,125	118,529	117,603	100,737	141,738	64,746	61,669	38,461
	F	114,159	120,117	83,396	98,914	43,200	61,775	12,123	35,287
	T	315,284	238,646	160,999	199,651	184,938	126,521	73,792	73,748

Table 4.6 Persons engaged and wages and salaries of employees, by nationality and major group of industrial activity

Major groups of industrial activity	Year	Employees				Persons engaged	
		Wages and salaries (KD)		Number			
		non-Kuwaiti	Kuwaiti	non-Kuwaiti	Kuwaiti	non-Kuwaiti	Kuwaiti
Fishing	1973	978 028	32 148	1 963	10	1 963	11
	1974	1 232 801	43 614	2 170	9	2 170	11
Crude petroleum and natural gas production	1973	5 992 268	3 852 197	2 301	1 291	2 303	2 291
	1974	7 369 581	4 752 625	2 325	1 350	2 328	1 351
Quarrying and other mining	1973	582 866	21 578	775	8	780	15
	1974	598 025	49 687	719	15	725	19
Food manufacturing	1973	1 948 551	52 540	2 814	19	3 373	44
	1974	2 221 090	66 484	2 856	15	3 295	26
Beverage industries	1973	662 794	7 822	9 944	2	946	4
	1974	762 096	8 563	1 093	2	1 095	6
Textiles	1973	98 855	–	196	–	249	5
	1974	93 302	–	153	–	217	11
Apparel except footwear	1973	2 162 646	600	2 471	1	3 848	20
	1974	1 948 831	–	2 619	–	4 023	13
Leather products; leather substitutes of fur, except footwear and wearing apparel	1973	18 615	–	30	–	31	1
	1974	8 880	–	13	–	16	–
Footwear except vulcanized or moulded rubber or plastic	1973	1 160	–	3	–	6	2
	1974	860	–	2	–	5	2

Wood and wood products except furniture	1973	996 902	4 200	1 056	1	1 078	9
	1974	722 517	5 250	952	1	982	6
Manufacture of furniture and fixtures, except primarily of metal	1973	800 125	–	1 171	–	1 744	16
	1974	1 037 649	3 932	1 256	3	1 871	20
Paper and paper products	1973	54 326	10 200	101	3	101	3
	1974	74 430	4 800	116	1	117	1
Printing, publishing products	1973	889 769	19 112	1 091	15	1 111	30
	1974	969 995	12 585	1 111	10	1 124	26
Industrial chemicals	1973	2 625 337	267 936	1 318	62	1 318	62
	1974	3 387 374	375 927	1 471	80	1 472	82
Other chemical products	1973	130 234	5 600	122	2	122	2
	1974	87 196	4 800	123	1	124	2
Petroleum refineries	1973	4 009 141	1 306 087	1 351	403	1 351	403
	1974	6 782 080	2 029 561	2 379	438	2 379	438
Miscellaneous products of petroleum and gas	1973	120 432	–	156	–	156	–
	1974	326 536	–	327	–	328	1
Rubber products	1973	30 302	–	56	–	62	1
	1974	62 130	–	69	–	73	2
Plastic products NEC	1973	72 059	1 320	120	1	120	4
	1974	74 633	1 867	107	2	107	5
Glass and glass products	1973	44 740	–	66	–	66	1
	1974	34 577	–	56	–	57	–
Non-metallic mineral products	1973	1 954 227	109 615	3 024	42	3 145	59
	1974	2 156 498	203 664	2 932			70

| Major groups of industrial activity | Year | Employees | | | | Persons engaged | |
| | | Wages and salaries (KD) | | Number | | | |
		non-Kuwaiti	Kuwaiti	non-Kuwaiti	Kuwaiti	non-Kuwaiti	Kuwaiti
Iron & steel basic industries	1973	259 520	10 200	395	3	401	?
	1974	433 675	29 650	519	6	522	6
Non-ferrous metal basic	1973	5 085	—	9	—	16	—
	1974	3 530	—	6	—	10	—
Fabricated metal products except machinery equipment	1973	1 585 698	3 168	2 366	1	2 704	20
	1974	1 803 201	5 445	2 303	1	2 585	13?
Machinery except electrical	1973	563 584	—	957	—	1 060	4
	1974	790 546	—	1 187	—	1 284	3
Electrical machinery, apparatus, appliances and supplies	1973	253 811	16 964	296	5	319	5
	1974	109 216	4 032	115	1	153	1
Transport equipment	1973	187 884	—	281	—	303	7
	1974	314 463	—	429	—	447	4
Other manufacturing industries	1973	154 447	—	191	—	254	1
	1974	161 131	—	176	—	246	4
Electricity, gas and steam	1973	2 040	—	7	—	16	—
	1974	10 340	3 000	14	2	22	3?
Total*	1973	26 206 418	5 689 139	23 669	1 859	26 983	2 011
	1974	32 344 322	7 561 872	25 428	1 986	28 653	2 115

Source: Central Statistical Office, Annual Statistical Abstract, Ministry of Planning, Kuwait, 1977, p. 18.

*Excluding Fishing

sector. The dualism in this case is between Kuwaitis and non-Kuwaitis on the one hand and between female and male on the other. Table 4.5 reflects several facts. First, it shows that the non-Kuwaiti element in the total labour force has exceeded the number of Kuwaitis in almost all sectors of the economy for the past twenty years. At the time of the 1975 census, the highest number of non-Kuwaitis was to be found in the services sector. The second largest employer of non-Kuwaitis was the wholesale and retail trade sector. The construction sector was a close third. Interestingly enough, the oil sector, in spite of its high contribution to GDP (more than 70 per cent) was the fourth largest employer in the economy. This is because of its capital-intensive nature.

As far as the sex composition of the labour force is concerned the number of males exceeds the number of females in almost all economic activities. The number of active Kuwaiti females in the labour force was 7,305 in 1975, while that for the non-Kuwaitis was more than 27,000. The percentage of inactive Kuwaiti females in relation to total Kuwaiti females in the labour force is about 87 per cent; that for the non-Kuwaiti females is about 75.4 per cent. Both percentages clearly indicate the small contribution made by the female elements of the population to the total labour force and consequently to the growth of the economy.

(d) Dualism in the salary and wages structure

The third feature of dualism is manifested in the wages and salaries structure of the labour force in Kuwait. The difference in income between Kuwaitis and non-Kuwaitis is high in almost all the major industrial activities. The Kuwaitis earn higher salaries and wages than the non-Kuwaitis, despite the fact that the latter group is much more highly qualified. Table 4.6 shows in detail the total wages and salaries accruing to Kuwaitis and non-Kuwaitis in all kinds of industrial economic activity, and illustrates the point. In the fishing sector in 1974 the total wages and salaries for non-Kuwaitis was KD1,232,801. The number of non-Kuwaitis employed in that sector was 2,170. The average wage and salary therefore works out at about KD568 a year. Compare this with the average income for Kuwaitis in that sector at about KD3,964. However, in the sector on crude-petroleum and natural-gas production the average income of non-Kuwaitis is much higher than Kuwaitis. This is because European and American technicians are employed, because their expertise is needed, and they usually enjoy higher salaries and also fringe benefits. In the food-manufacturing sectors the general average income of the non-Kuwaitis is KD674, while that of the Kuwaitis is about KD2,557. In summary, the total industrial wages and salaries for the non-Kuwaiti population in industry was about KD32,344,332 in 1974 and the number of persons engaged in that sector of the non-Kuwaiti element of the industrial labour force was about 28,653. This yields an average annual income of about KD1,477.8 as against KD3,575.3 for Kuwaitis.

Table 4.6 shows the breakdown of all the components of the industrial sector corresponding to the number of Kuwaitis and non-Kuwaitis employed and engaged in sub-sectors. The same kind of dichotomy applies in all sectors of the economy — agriculture as well as construction and the wholesale and retail trade. It is also evident in the private and public sectors. These facts cannot be reconciled with the idea that GNP per cent per capita income is very high — as is frequently suggested by the press and some financial agents, who take no account of the actual distribution of income but depend solely on the division of the value of total GNP by the total number of the population.

(e) Surpluses and gaps

In addition to the structural dualism of the economy in general and the labour force in particular, the Kuwaiti economy is characterized by three kinds of surplus and gap. The first gap is between government revenue and government expenditure, resulting in a surplus for almost every year. The second gap is in the international trade balance, where there is always a surplus in the balance of payments. The third gap is in savings and investment, where a higher percentage of GNP is saved. However, more than half the amount saved is invested domestically.

1 Revenue-expenditure gap

Table 4.7 shows that the government realized a surplus almost every year from 1957 to 1977. The general budget deficits in 1966-7 and 1967-8 were mainly due to sharp increases in government expenditure on almost all fronts. Expenditure on land purchase was increasing as well as expenditure on capital development. In addition, there were other outside commitments to the United Arab Command and the Palestine Liberation Organization. The highest budget surplus was

Table 4.7 *Estimated government revenue and expenditu*
(KD millions)

Year	Government revenue	Government expenditure	
1957	122.85	88.82	
1958	146.51	116.45	30.06
1959	172.51	143.28	29.23
1960-1	183.45	135.08	48.37
1961-2	192.89	161.65	31.24
1962-3	202.07	163.59	38.48
1963-4	208.08	189.79	18.29
1964-5	222.0	182.1	39.9
1965-6	243.7	234.2	9.5
1966-7	248.1	299.3	- 51.2
1967-8	285.2	287.4	- 2.2
1968-9	258.7	258.5	0.2
1969-70	306.54		
1970-1	373.9	303.2	70.7
1971-2	424.0	346.9	77.1
1972-3	597.7	396.7	201.0
1973-4	675.3*	536.7	138.6
1974-5	2,271.4	1,085.2	1,186.2
1975-6	3,224.4†	1,337.4	1,887.0
1976-7	3,033.1‡	1,519.3	1,513.8
1977-8	2,569.9	2,125.2	444.7

Source: Ministry of Finance, Kuwait.

* Fiscal year from 1 April to the end of March.
† Exceptional fiscal year from 1 April to the end of June.
‡ Fiscal year from 1 July to the end of June.

realized in 1975-6 as a result of increasing oil prices and the government takeover of the remaining share of KOC. The surplus was KD1,887 million – and that is net of public expenditure, which includes current domestic expenditure, land purchases, development, local loans, contributions to shares of local companies and financial institutions and foreign transfer. Even after all these huge disbursements were made by the Kuwaiti government, for domestic expenditure and to foreign governments, there remained a large amount of accumulated capital surplus invested abroad. The Kuwaiti government's total foreign investment is in the region of $25 billion. This will lead in the coming few years to a large investment income as another source of wealth for Kuwait apart from oil.

Government foreign investment is in short-term deposits in US, European and Japanese banks. Large amounts of money are invested in government securities and equities. It is the policy of the government

Table 4.8 *International balance of payments, 1975–7*

Description	1977 Preliminary Debit	1977 Preliminary Credit	1976 Debit	1976 Credit	1975 Debit	1975 Credit
1 GOODS AND SERVICES (NET)		1,900		2,196		2,019
Trade Balance		1,712		1,897		1,794
Exports and Re-exports (fob)		2,784		2,828		2,459
of which: oil and gas exports		(2,587)		(2,615)		(2,289)
Imports (fob)	1,072		931		655	
Non-monetary gold	53	2	34	2	32	2
Services (Net)		239		331		255
Freight and insurance	169	17	126	29	91	5
Other transportation	39	118	35	102	33	81
Travel	153	41	73	30	59	24
Investment income	56	548	36	477	38	372
Government	(–)	(258)	(–)	(255)	(–)	(173)
Financial institutions	(43)	(125)	(20)	(82)	(12)	(72)
Other private	(13)	(165)	(16)	(140)	(26)	(127)
Other government (not classified)	67	11	38	9	30	7
Other services	15	3	13	5	7	4
2 PRIVATE TRANSFERS	106	–	92	–	80	–
3 TOTAL CURRENT ACCOUNT (1 + 3)		1,794		2,104		1,939
4 NON-MONETARY CAPITAL AND OFFICIAL TRANSFERS (NET):*	348	–	1268		792	
Official transfers	231		65		230	
Direct investment	32		177		47	
Government	(20)		(85)		(20)	
Kuwait Fund	(7)		(17)		(6)	
Other investment institutions	(5)		(15)		(21)	

Loans (Net)	49	(8)	35	(6)	11	(7)
Kuwait Fund	(55)	(37)	(49)	(44)	(22)	(16)
Other investment institutions	(39)		(36)		(12)	
Other non-monetary capital	18		442		288	(58)
Oil sector		(76)	(221)			
Government	(56)		(149)		(185)	
Kuwait Fund	(23)		(5)		(91)	
Investment institutions	(24)	(11)	(17)		(32)	
Specialized banks	(37)	(35)	(50)		(38)	
Other private sector†	18		609		210	
5 COMMERCIAL BANKS (NET)						
Liabilities	52	96		94	27	26
Assets	148		–	–	53	–
Total (3 + 4 + 5)		1,394	61			
6 RESERVES AND REVEALED ITEMS						
Central Bank of Kuwait (Assets)	1,394		930		1,120	
Monetary gold	69		63		92	
Reserve position in IMF		(38)	(20)	(–)	(6)	(–)
Other assets		(8)	(48)	(–)	(112)	(–)
Ministry of Finance‡	(315)		(–)	(15)	(–)	(26)
	1,125	867	867		1,028	

* Increases in assets or decreases in liabilities are debit items while decreases in assets or increases in liabilities are credit items.

† Residual item, reflecting partly errors and omissions, but mostly outflow of private capital.

‡ Estimate based on available information for the period 31 March 1975–31 January 1976 for 1976, but actuals for the full year of 1977.

not to take over companies completely. Sensitivity to the foreign press, governments and the public is one reason for this; another, important, reason is that the government requires such managerial expertise in the international environment. Finally, it is important to be discreet, an essential base for portfolio management.

2 The international balance of payments: an overall surplus

The Kuwaiti financial authorities have not yet compiled accurate official figures on Kuwait's international balance of payments. However, there are certain figures, prepared by the Research Department of the Kuwaiti Central Bank, that are useful. Table 4.8 shows that the balance of payments for 1977 is similar to that for 1976, with the exception of the declining trend in the trade and current surpluses in 1977. Nevertheless an overall surplus was realized by the increase of foreign reserves. The decline in the current-account surplus of 1977 was mainly due to the decrease in the trade and services surplus, because of zero increase in government foreign-investment income, large payments for freight and insurance and the increasing rate of travel expenditure. In spite of this, the overall surplus in the balance of payments remained the main feature mainly because of the oil-sector item under 'Non-monetary Capital' – this item shifting from debit position as a result of the 60-day credit period allowed by the Ministry of Oil for the settlements of oil-purchase contracts. Another item which increased the overall surplus in 1977 was the decrease in government balances with the central banks of the Arab countries, from KD149 million in 1976 to KD56 million in 1977.

The balance-of-trade statistics indicate that the ratio of Kuwaiti foreign-trade GDP is very high (around 87 per cent for 1975). This is probably one of the highest ratios in the world. Oil exports stood at around 91 per cent of total exports in 1977 as against 92 per cent in 1976. The explanation for the decline in 1977 could be found in the decrease in oil production and a substantial increase in the value of non-oil exports despite the fact that there was a 10 per cent increase in oil prices at the beginning of that year. If oil exports are excluded, then chronic deficits will take root in the economy and imports, which range from food to luxurious cars and goods, which at the present time are financed by oil receipts through government expenditure, will cease to flow into the country.

3 National savings versus domestic investment

National savings have been increasing since 1957. However, the increase was more dramatic in the 1970s, as shown in Table 4.9. National savings increased from KD220.4 million in 1970-1 to KD2,006.8 million in 1975-6. The average annual increase during that period was about 1.82 per cent. This was mainly due to the increase in proceeds from oil exports, ascribed to higher oil and gas prices rather than to an increase in oil production itself. Consequently, national savings reached 22.93 per cent of the GDP in 1970-1. By the end of 1975-6 national savings represented 61.2 per cent of the GDP. This could be considered one of the highest percentages in the world.

The rate of increase in the net purchase of invisible foreign assets was even more dramatic than the increase in national savings over the same period. They increased from KD121.4 million in 1970-1 to KD1,851.2 million in 1975-6. They increased by a factor of 15, which gives an average annual increase of about 2.2 per cent over the period 1970-6. An interesting fact is revealed by the data of Table 4.9 for local capital formation in comparison with the figures corresponding to depreciation of fixed assets. The fact is that local capital formation is not much more than depreciation, which means very little is added to the productive capabilities of the economy. In brief, the role of the government and the private sector during 1970-6 was a replacement role rather than an additional one as far as capital formation was concerned. The question is why this has been happening in a capital-surplus country with great growth potential. Chapter 5 will attempt to answer that question as briefly as possible, whereby the concept of the limited absorptive capacity of the economy is completely refuted.

Recapitulation

The preceding section shows the dualistic nature of the Kuwaiti economy, between an efficient oil industry, and the much less efficient traditional sector. Dualism is also manifested in the labour force, i.e. there are more foreigners than there are natives on all fronts of economic activity. Male-female dualism is also apparent in the insignificant economic role of the female in general, regardless of nationality. In addition to structural dualism the Kuwaiti economy has been characterized by surpluses and gaps on three fronts: between government revenues and government expenditure; in overall surplus in the balance of payments;

Table 4.9 *Savings and investments (KD millions)*

Items	1970-1	1971-2	1972-3	1973-4	1974-5	1975-6
Government capital formation	62.6	71.5	101.6	92.8	112.9	135.7
Private capital formation	46.5	48.0	51.7	53.9	63.0	106.6
Change in stocks	0.8	1.0	1.3	(1.0)	6.7	9.3
Net invisible asset: purchases from abroad	121.4	252	275.5	729.6	1,770.6	1,851.2
Net loans to the outside world	(2.7)	(3.1)	9.7	(0.6)	20.1	64.0
Statistical errors		66	41.4	6.1	28.5	50.0
TOTAL ACCUMULATION	228.6	435.4	481.2	880.8	2,001.8	2,220.8
Depreciation of fixed assets	108.4	116.5	120.1	142.8	177.4	188
Savings	220.4	343.7	474.2	862.5	1,780.8	2,006.8
Net capital transfer from outside	(100.2)	(24.8)	(113.1)	(124.5)	43.6	2.6
Financing foreign capital accumulation	228.6	435.4	481.2	880.8	2,001.8	2,220.8

Source: General Department for Planning, 'An Analytical Study of Kuwaiti National Income Account', Ministry of Planning, 1977, Kuwait, p. 25.

100

and in the high rate of savings invested abroad, amounting to a very high percentage of total saving and national income. The persistence of these surpluses cannot be attributed to the limited absorptive capacity of the country, nor to the unavailability of government projects. The IBRD missions thought they had found reasons in the lack of natural resources but they forgot to consider the hundreds of oil and gas derivatives. Although it may be true that Kuwait lacks natural resources other than oil and gas, nevertheless there are several other factors that stand as obstacles to the use of capital surplus for economic development. A more realistic approach to this problem lies in the realm of socio-economic and political factors which inhibit the emergence of the imaginative entrepreneur and discourage the rise of the creative public administrator and government manager. The factors do not encourage the emergence of the desired change in the structure of the economy.

Chapter 5

Limiting factors

Economic lines of thought

Economists are *à la mode*. In the eighteenth and nineteenth centuries, economists were concerned with economic progress (except for Marx, who was mainly concerned with the decline of the capitalist system). Each of them stressed certain aspects of economic development. Adam Smith considered the right institutional framework as an important factor in economic progress. Malthus put more emphasis on a low valuation of income in relation to leisure, while David Ricardo was interested in distribution rather than growth. Almost all economists have stressed the importance of technology. Marx, however, gave more weight to the importance of technology as a function of investment. Nevertheless, for sociological reasons he predicted the breakdown of capitalism. He recognized capitalism as an 'engine of growth'. With a quaint touch of teleology Marx said repeatedly that 'it is the "historical task" or privilege of capitalist society to create a productive apparatus that will be adequate for the requirements of a higher form of human civilization.'[1]

In the twentieth century, economists began to point out specific factors hindering or facilitating economic growth. Schumpeter was very much concerned with the role of the entrepreneur as a good qualitative element in the population of any country, able to lead the economy to a higher stage of economic growth. He considered the absence of the entrepreneur, or his decline, as a reason for the decline of the capitalist system. McClelland has put more emphasis on the psychological factor. His hypothesis states that 'a society with a generally high level of N-achievement will produce more energetic entrepreneurs who, in turn, produce more rapid economic development'.[2] Hagan deals with a broader field — with the complexities of the social psychology of certain cultures and societies. His interdisciplinary approach makes his explanation and reasoning for economic development more encompassing. To him: 'since the economic state of society is closely related to its political state and the forces that bring change in the one also bring some sort of change in the other, a model that explains economic growth must take into account non-economic as well as economic aspects of human behaviour.'[3]

The late-twentieth-century economists have drawn unclear, vague lines, dividing themselves into two separate groups. One group puts more emphasis on capital, the other on labour, as the determining factor in economic development. Lewis gave more weight to the latter, while Robinson at Cambridge gave more importance to the former. This kind of choice between capital and labour usually reflects a state of mind of ideological difference.

Radical economists — represented by Dobb, Sweezy, Baran and Robinson — give more weight to capital investment. However, they have stressed the primacy of political and social factors. Nevertheless: 'The accumulation of capital is the most effective way to create the other conditions required for economic growth; these requisites are created concurrently with and primarily by a high rate of capital formation.'[4] Non-radical economists, such as Johnson, give weight to other factors such as rationality, responsiveness, and the right institutional framework for a capitalist system, rather than capital accumulation alone. In the words of Johnson:[5]

Industrialization requires far more than the investment of capital in the establishment of industrial facilities in the 'infrastructure' (roads, railways, docks, the generation and transmission of electric power, etc.) required to power them and link them to markets. Among its obvious requirements are the development of a skilled, disciplined, and acquisitively motivated labour force and the creation of a professional managerial class able to combine disciplined teamwork with imaginative entrepreneurship.

Chapter 3 of this book shows that foreign capital and technology have provided the Kuwaiti economy with massive capital that should have been conducive to social and economic development. Despite this fact, the Kuwaiti economy has been unable to transfer itself from a dualistic economy depending wholly on oil export to a diversified economy. This chapter tries to reconcile the difference between the importance of capital accumulation and the importance of a disciplined and acquisitively motivated labour force. The main factors limiting the ability of the Kuwaiti economy to change its structure can be located in the nature of the labour force and in the political, social and economic institutions.

The political and social framework

Figure 5.1 shows the power relations in the Kuwaiti political set-up. and suggests how these influences may be used to resolve internal power conflicts that cannot be resolved satisfactorily in parliament and which may otherwise lead to problems on a national scale.

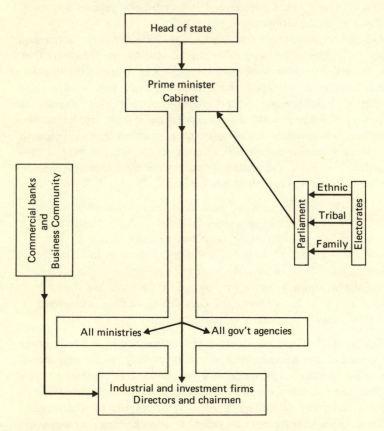

Figure 5.1 *Power relations in Kuwait*

The head of state appoints a prime minister, who in turn forms a cabinet (which can be subject to a vote of no confidence in parliament). The prime minister also appoints undersecretaries and directors of government agencies. The prime minister thus has great influence and he is able to use this influence to resolve possible conflicts. Power conflicts based on tribal, ethnic or family origins would best be resolved through his selection of his cabinet, while his influence in appointing undersecretaries and heads of government agencies is a second means of resolving all sorts of power conflicts. A third means is available through government influence in industry and investment, since the government has shares in most of the industrial and investment firms.

Political parties in Kuwait are forbidden by constitution — the government will always have the power and control. As a result, social and political groups identify themselves on ethnic, tribal and family affiliations. This effectively precludes the national political integration that is necessary for a national identity in Kuwait and for its national development.

That such extensive power in the hands of the prime minister has remained unchallenged may be attributed to the connection between politics and economics in Kuwait. Unlike many countries of the world, collection of public revenue is independent of the people, the banks and the business community. The government is rich and has huge reserves of hard currency. Its revenue comes directly from the foreign oil companies holding concessions in Kuwait and it now owns almost all the oil companies in Kuwait. There is, however, a mutual political awareness between the business community and the government of Kuwait, despite the economic independence of the latter, for by not adopting certain measures that would be unpopular with the business community the government can, of course, retain its support.

There are two main social factors that hinder rapid industrialization. Firstly, the extended family system discourages individuals from working, saving or investing. In low-income countries where social welfare is a rare policy, the extended family system provides the advantages of social security to its individuals. In Kuwait, however, which enjoys a high per capita inome coupled with a policy of social security and aid, the extended family system is a hindrance to economic growth. The head of a family who owns a business usually appoints his son and the latter appoints his relatives in different branches of the business. Such a policy clearly does not ensure the most efficient, ambitious and suitably qualified managers that are so badly needed for the national development of Kuwait.

The second factor is the closed social system in Kuwait. Assimilation through marriage or horizontal mobility is restricted by family and tribal bars. Social status within the community is the all-important criterion. Because of these social values and beliefs, occupational mobility on the basis of ascription rather than achievement is the rule.

Government management

The problem of administration began for Kuwait as early as 1946, when the government began to receive its first revenue from oil exports. At that time Kuwait had no organized administration or sound budgetary system. There was no expertise available in modern public administration, planning, budgeting and the other tools so necessary for effective modern management. There was no co-ordination between the various government departments, and duplication of work and cost was the norm. Recruitment within government departments was made on the traditional basis of tribal, family or ethnic loyalties.

The result of all this was a foregone conclusion: financial and administrative chaos. Financial mismanagement and waste were widespread and though a central tender committee was set up to minimize this it became institutionalized on a large scale.

(It ought to be stated, however, that despite this situation many hospitals, a number of schools and hundreds of kilometres of roads were built in Kuwait and by the end of the 1950s Kuwait was a visibly different country from that which it had been in 1946. The era could be said to have been characterized by rapid change but without any specific planning policy.)

This financial mismanagement of the national economy did not pass unnoticed and a number of political issues was raised in Kuwait. The press took an increasing interest and later it became its daily theme. Political organizations began to gain in popularity and underground movements were encouraged by their rising numbers of recruits.

This increasing political opposition was encouraged by the desire and the will for political representation. The opposition was first suppressed by force and some of the leaders were put under temporary house arrest and their passports withheld. These internal tensions were reinforced by the pan-Arab nationalist movement that was infiltrating almost all Arab countries. Their aim was Arab unity in one state. However, the political organizations concerned were unsure of the means to achieve this and of the political and economic system required to serve it.

The late Amir, Shaikh Abdula Al-Salem Al-Sabah, was aware of the aspirations of the various political factions in Kuwait. He was constantly reminded of the political uprisings of 1938, in which he had played a great role. During the late 1950s continuous consultation took place between the late Amir and the leaders of some of the political factions. These consultations centred on a representative system, which culminated in the establishment of the constituent assembly in 1961 and an elected parliament in 1963 (unfortunately dissolved on 29 August 1976). Kuwait enjoyed a few years of parliamentary life which brought a degree of rationality to the workings of the government and its various ministries. Control over the budget and expenditure was imposed and the general running of the economy was improved.

Nevertheless, the government administration was still unable to cope with the very rapid rate of development, and the lack of a satisfactory system hindered and delayed realization of the potentialities of economic growth in many other sectors of the economy.

The development that did take place was haphazard and was facilitated by the absence of financial constraints only. Projects were undertaken that would have benefited from a more careful examination of the social cost and benefit. The statistical record of the past twenty-five years is impressive from the point of view of the number of schools, hospitals and roads built, the increasing rate of government investment in the economy and consequently the large volume of government employees in relation to the total labour force. However, the drawbacks of that record are brought into even sharper focus by the lack of a clear, co-ordinated overall social and economic policy.

Present-day administration

It is still the case that there is a need for an integrated management system from top to bottom and for a proper logistics system to deal with the complexities of planning and organization. Any attempt at modern administration is still hampered by traditional ways of dealing with matters. The Council of Ministers does not have the specialists or the specialized support organizations necessary to deal with planning, resource allocation, budgeting and the various sectors of government manpower — yet these are the foundations of an effective and efficient modern management.

The problems of the various individual ministries reflect some of the greatest needs. Some ministers have neither the training nor the practical experience their positions demand. Their refusal to delegate may aggravate matters, with disastrous results — work congestion, chaos, inefficient management and public discontent and political complaints. Yet even when a well-qualified minister is appointed there may be a different type of problem to face: he may wish to delegate power but may find that there is reluctance to accept the responsibility because of a heavy commitment to private commercial activities. This means overworked ministers and an even louder public outcry for reform.

The above problems are reinforced by an absence of co-ordination between ministries and a lack of co-operation among the departments within ministries. Each ministry has a purchasing department yet some ministries might have used their allocated funds for certain equipment while others may not have used their funds at all. Accounting co-ordination is supposed to solve this problem but in Kuwait any department showing a financial deficit has to wait a year to buy its equipment — and what makes the problem even worse is that the equipment may well be there, unused in another ministry's warehouse. This sort of problem usually arises in ministries or government bodies that have similar functional objectives but lack co-ordination. The cost to the nation is enormous both in terms of money and time.

Planning

Planning is an integral part of national development whereby natural, financial and human resources are used efficiently and effectively — yet an adequate planning policy does not exist in Kuwait. It must be said that there is a Ministry of Planning with various departments, among which the statistical office is probably one of the best in the Middle East. Nevertheless, economic planning in the sense that priorities and goals are established and the means by which they are to be achieved are stated does not exist. There is a five-year plan but it is indicative rather than an official policy plan. It is drawn up by foreign experts employed by the Ministry of Planning and is based on information collected on the aspirations of various ministries. The real problems are not stated explicitly, such as manpower and population policy. The consequences are naturally grave. The government is trying to diversify the economy but it does not say how it is going to do this and which sections should be given priority. This is normally decided by the prime minister or by the Amir, which is not national economic planning. What makes matters even worse in Kuwait is that plans might be accepted by the Ministry of Commerce and Industry on economic grounds only to be rejected by the Council of Ministers on political grounds or for other unspecified reasons.

Population planning

The absence of a clear population policy has meant that Kuwait City's projected population for the year 2000 has already been surpassed. The estimated figure for the year 2000 was about 95,000 people. The present number of people living and working in Kuwait City is about 290,000. The same is also true for the projected population growth in the suburbs. The result is a congested capital with traffic jams and a high number of accidents.

Roads between the capital and suburbs and other governorates also suffer from this problem and they are increasingly unable to cope with the rising number of cars. The high population also means that schools and hospitals are overcrowded and that housing for the needy Kuwaitis and the newly naturalized Bedouins is becoming a rarity. The problem becomes more complex with the increasing number of immigrants and the consequent rise in rents.

Budget planning

Prior to independence and the establishment of the National Assembly, funds were allocated to the various departments without any formal budgeting procedures. There was no guarantee that budget allocators would govern actual expenditure. The system of accounting was not the same for all departments — it was left to chief accountants within each department to decide upon the method employed. There were no formal auditing procedures and expenditure was based on that of a previous year.

Even after the introduction of the parliamentary system in 1963, budgeting procedures changed little. Though some parliamentarians were genuinely concerned about the costs of financing projects, others were more concerned with fiscal bargaining at the expense of budgeting effectiveness and priority projects. It was little wonder that the government used the delaying of approval of certain projects as a pretext for the dissolution of parliament on 29 August 1976.

Budgeting still remains unsophisticated and is hindered by the large number of committees the members of which are not versed in fiscal planning and the requirements of national development, which demand the allocation of national resources nationally and with a futuristic outlook. Even after dissolution of parliament nothing was done to impose budgeting procedures. Each department blames the other for this – it is a vicious circle to which there is no end. Private companies are hired to carry out feasibility studies yet no firm objectives exist. Without the availability of demographic and socio-economic data and a clear purpose, planning and budgeting become impossible if fruitful results are anticipated.

National planning

The lack of a clearly specified strategic plan for the whole nation is another problem facing government political administrators. Announcements that economic growth and diversification of the economy, more equitable distribution of income, more and better housing and schools, are to be achieved shortly are often heard but the policies adopted are discouraging rather than accelerating the realization of these objectives.

Economic structure has not changed for quite some time. The oil sector still provides more than 90 per cent of government revenue and more than 75 per cent of the GNP. Although there are several government institutions encouraging growth in industry, such as Shuaiba industrial area and the Industrial Bank of Kuwait, the Ministry of Commerce and Industry and the Ministry of Finance, there is a need for greater co-ordination among them. Political policies and objectives regarding the limit on how much Kuwait should accept foreigners inside Kuwait also limit the achievement of the other objectives such as industrialization, which are often labour intensive. However, there are other industries that are less labour intensive, being mainly geared to services such as the growth of banks, investment and insurance companies. These must be encouraged to grow and the government should establish educational institutions to provide them with the necessary qualified manpower.

Education

Although Kuwait has more than thirty years of systematic education the supply of professional and skilled manpower is very limited. There is a Central Training Department, which belongs to the Ministry of Labour and Social Affairs, but the number of students under training is limited. The Telecommunications Training Institute and the Shuaikh Industrial Training Centre both belong to the Central Training Department and are supposed to turn out skilled manpower, but the Ministry of Education does not recognise their certificates as sufficient for higher studies.

The problem of skilled manpower is reinforced by the social outlook towards the technical and vocational professions. This kind of attitude is not only limited to Kuwait but covers almost all the Arab countries, for very deep cultural reasons. Likewise, the Ministry of Health is actively planning for more hospitals and clinics but is doing little about the manpower to run them. There is a lack of hospital administrators in all kinds of categories. A common strategy between the Ministry of Education and the Ministry of Health regarding the supply and demand for doctors, nurses, pharmacists and other technical medical staff, would provide a major step towards solving this problem.

Public administration

Public administration in Kuwait is another area where improvement could be made. Reducing manpower and improving efficiency would help accelerate the implementation of national programmes, reduce costs and help improve resource-allocation patterns. There is a need also for training centres that provide a sound training in the serious practical problems of public administration. Although there is an Arab Planning Institute, which runs a public administration and industrial management department, its programmes are theoretically based.

There is a further problem in that many of the best public administrators are gradually leaving the government sector to join the private sector, which promises higher salaries and greater promotion prospects.

The solution to these administrative problems is made all the more difficult by the Civil Service Employment Act of 1960, which is still in force. It is rigid and outdated and has made the dismissal of Kuwaiti and non-Kuwaiti public servants alike virtually impossible. If these problems and their consequences are to be solved then political decisions to reform the government administration and its regulations must be forthcoming.

Management in the private and semi-private sector

Good management has traditionally been one of the abilities of the Kuwaiti entrepreneur. This was particularly apparent in the pre-oil economy of Kuwait. Today, however, management is very much the domain of the non-Kuwaiti. This change has not been the result of any inability in modern Kuwaitis but has rather been an evolving process in the post-oil development of Kuwait.

The first chapter of the book illustrated the importance of the sea-faring and pearl-diving industries as the main pillars of the pre-oil economy of Kuwait. These were prosperous industries in which management was an important and influential factor in their growth and development. The working population possessed certain specific skills and worked hard. They acquired these skills through on-the-job training. The managers worked even harder, for in most cases they were the owners of the ships, whether of the seafaring or pearl-diving variety. They managed the crews, the finance, the sea and trade routes. Their success was similar to the Scandinavian private tanker owners during the heyday of the oil-tanker market. Their main natural assets were the geographical location of Kuwait and its access via land and sea.

With the discovery and subsequent export of oil, the two main industries declined. The older managers and owners survived, however, with their traditional methods of management. They continued to engage in trade, but mainly as agents and importers. This time, however, there was no need to work so hard: monopoly possession based on sole agencies and effective demand for their products worked for them. As a result there was a phenomenal growth in their businesses and because of this they had to depend on other managers, and mainly on expatriate ones. Though they educated their sons abroad, mainly in the UK and USA, they did not allow them sufficient responsibility in running their businesses. In addition, the death of some of the old owners meant freedom and independence for their young educated sons as a result of inherited wealth.

A situation was arrived at where it became almost normal for most kinds of private business to be managed by non-Kuwaitis.

Important to this set-up was the fact that Kuwaiti business owners do not like to employ Kuwaiti managers because they do not like to instruct them, which might lead to disagreement and perhaps eventually to the loss of a friend. They are keen to have them as close, intimate friends; they accept advice from them but they do not wish to have them as permanent managers. Second, and most important culturally, is the fact that Kuwaiti businessmen do not wish other Kuwaitis to know the nature of their business or the extent of their profitability.

The presence of such non-Kuwaiti businessmen and managers, however, helped some of the present wealthy business families to accrue their wealth. Because non-Kuwaitis cannot legally own businesses in Kuwait unless they are in joint venture with Kuwaitis, some of the initiating ideas for establishing businesses have come from non-Kuwaiti businessmen and managers, who have had similar businesses themselves in other countries or who have seen such ideas exploited effectively in those countries. Usually in such circumstances the Kuwaitis accept part-ownership but leave the management side to the non-Kuwaitis. The role of the Kuwaiti partner is to facilitate the continued growth of the venture through his various contacts and through general public-relations activities.

Of course, Kuwaiti businessmen do also initiate various business ideas. Often, however, and particularly when they are employed in the government or the semi-private sector, they may wish to limit their involvement to a purely financial one, seeing their position primarily in prestigious terms (rather than as a source of income), to help facilitate their private business interests.

Whilst Kuwaitis, therefore, are frequently not involved in management directly, it should not be supposed that they are thereby less competent as managers than non-Kuwaitis: possession of various technical skills does not ensure good management capabilities. However, there is a need for greater emphasis on the right kind of management education and training for Kuwaitis, a vital requirement for the continued national development of Kuwait.

There is plenty of room for improvement and increased productivity within the private sector but one of the problems is the unusually high rates of return, which means that there is little motivation for either Kuwaiti or non-Kuwaiti managers to work harder (though feelings of insecurity among non-Kuwaitis probably causes them to work harder for more available transferable money). The high rates of return usually emanate from import activities, where profit margins are very high.

Another sector from which large amounts of profit have been made

113

is the construction sector among local contractors. However, several productive economic activities remain disorganized – for example, plumbing, electrical installation work, printing, painting and maintenance – and need a greater co-ordination of their activities before they can improve their contribution to the private sector.

Although large segments of the population are involved in real-estate business, there is very little modern real-estate management and financing. Commercial real estate is mostly individually owned, with a consequent fragmentation. Also, there has been a great deal of speculation as a result of government land policy.

The private banks and investment companies are wholly Kuwaiti owned and are governed by Kuwaiti boards of directors. However, management is usually foreign and is increasingly by large foreign financial institutions. The private banks and investment companies can thus find themselves open to powerful influences, and which they may not always consider to be in their best interests.

It is worthy of note also that the private banks and investment companies do not insist in their contracts with the managing companies on a training programme for Kuwaiti nationals in banking and financial techniques and management. To do so would provide a valuable means of training Kuwaitis in these vital skills so necessary to the country's development.

Semi-private companies

As we have already seen, the joint sector forms an important part of the economic set-up in Kuwait. It allows the government to encourage the private sector to increase its role in development and to undertake investment in industries in which the government takes the initiative, and it provides the means to achieve social and socio-economic goals that might not be achieved by the private sector alone. Naturally in practice there are problems.

Managerial problems in the semi-private companies can be more difficult since both private and government interests are represented, and this can mean that the attendant managerial problems of both the public and private sectors are involved. The problems have been increasing with the number of semi-private companies and there have been examples of adverse consequences.

Government participation in joint-sector companies does, of course, reduce the risks involved for the private sector – this is part of the attraction. However, this can in itself be a problem in that companies may look upon the government's involvement as an 'umbrella' against failure, whereby they can seek subsequent compensation from the government in the event that matters fail. Examples of such an attitude have also meant that companies have not bothered to provide skilled training for Kuwaitis.

Another problem within the joint sector economy is the role of the board of directors. Some of the representatives of the private sector of the joint-stock companies feel that the present degree of involvement of the government does not allow them sufficient freedom, so that their companies in particular and the economy as a consequence suffer accordingly. Greater clarification of the government's ideas as to how it sees the role of its boards in joint ventures with the private sector is needed. If they are intended as functional bodies then naturally they must embody diverse experienced management personnel, each experienced and qualified in his own field. If, however, they are to be considered as policy-making bodies, then involvement may be of a more peripheral nature.

Private and semi-private companies listed on the Kuwaiti stock exchange are operating in conditions of complete or near monopoly. Such a lack of competition removes the incentive to reduce prices or to produce better products, classic features of a monopoly situation. This means high prices for the consumer in particular and the cost to the nation in general is high.

Within the joint-sector economy there is a need for greater clarification of overall planning policy, of both long- and short-term objectives, and for greater co-ordination and organization. Efficient planning is essential, to ensure that there are sound reasons for the establishing of companies and to ensure that there is the most effective use of manpower, and that there is no duplication of cost and effort, with a subsequent waste of the skilled manpower so vital to Kuwait. It may be advisable that the government introduce safeguards and regulations conditional to the granting of financial help, to ensure the realization of future benefits to the nation — in Kuwaiti there are no such safeguards at present yet almost all the governments in the world have such regulations. And the government should encourage the growth of private and semi-private companies. It is the proliferation of such companies that leads to the growth of the primary and secondary capital markets, that leads to the development of better managerial capabilities with an international outlook, and that not only sharpens efficiency through competition but also creates opportunities abroad and enhances co-operation.

Economic institutions

(a) Efforts and rewards

A fundamental mechanism in every human society is rewarded effort. Unfortunately, Kuwaiti society lacks such a mechanism. This is mainly because the distribution of a large part of the oil revenue to the population was uneven and failed to stimulate productive domestic investment. As discussed in chapter 3, the land-purchase programme was considered by the government an ideal method for the distribution of income, and from the very beginning, therefore, a large part of the population received money without having to work for it. This has also created a feeling of complete dependence on the government as an ideal method for the distribution of income.

Coupled with the enjoyment of free medical and educational services, without taxes at an earlier stage of national development, most Kuwaitis could not see a relationship between their rewards and their efforts, mainly because they were not expecting them and therefore were not working for them. Nevertheless, many Kuwaitis in the private sector have worked very hard and have enjoyed the rewards of their work.

Another area of disconnected relations between reward and effort is exemplified in the dichotomy of the Kuwaiti population. Foreigners, who comprise more than 54 per cent of the population, do not have the right to own property or to start commercial businesses on their own. The labour market deliberately discriminates between the Kuwaitis and non-Kuwaitis.

It was Professor Arthur Lewis who emphasized the importance of a rewarded effort and its role in economic development. He wrote that *'Men will not make an effort unless the fruit of that effort is assured to themselves or to those whose claims they recognize.'*[6] Since Kuwaitis are usually paid higher rates than non-Kuwaitis with the same qualifications and experience, this policy creates a double standard. This kind of feeling discourages people from working and consequently discourages economic development and growth.

It is well known that any social system is able to change itself if it gets the right institutions and the resources so that everybody is rewarded according to his work and effort. That does not mean that everybody will get the same benefit, because people are endowed with different capabilities and intelligence. It is competition that might bring differential payments closer.

(b) The nature of the oil concessions in Kuwait

Chapter 2 analysed the oil concessions in Kuwait. The main points were: payments per barrel were low compared to other oil-producing countries; the area covered by the concessions is very large compared with leased areas in the western and eastern hemispheres; the duration of KOC's concession in Kuwait is the longest on record (92 years); and all the oil companies in Kuwait refine a minute quantity compared to the volume of crude oil exported. It is this latter point which acts as an obstacle to industrial expansion and diversification in Kuwait. The whole range of the petrochemical industries depends on the availability of oil refineries and of gas. The limited amount of oil refined cannot be explained by location theory or by the dictates of the theory of international trade.

Location theory

There is no doubt that the existence and location of different industries in different regions constitutes a problem which needs a scientific explanation. Logically speaking, our solution to this problem lies in finding connections and order among facts. That order could be achieved if the hypothesis, which is offered as a solution to the problem at hand, is capable of being verified empirically. Location has been a tentative explanation to the problem at hand. That explanation was suggested to location theorists by something in the subject matter and by their previous knowledge. It proved to be a good explanation for the phenomena they wanted to explain by testing the consequences of their hypothesis against experience directly.

Location theory is a new branch of economics. It acts as a link between industrial economics and industrial engineering. Industries follow locational principles in evolutionary fashion because factors affecting location of industries are always changing and science adds new factors which make the variables affecting location of industries so diverse that it is impossible to predict locational trends.

To explain location theory, one might assume a single case where a commodity is made from one raw material only. Under such an assumption the commodity produced might be source-orientated, market-orientated or footloose. Source-orientated industries are located near the sources of raw materials because they are weight-losing or weight-saving in the course of processing or manufacturing. To locate such kinds of industries near the source reduces the processing cost by getting rid of a large element of cost (transportation).

Market-orientated industries are those which produce goods and commodities of a perishable nature. It is also true that industries in which processing adds weight or bulk to the product are produced closer to the market in order to reduce processing costs. This is done by eliminating transportation costs that would otherwise be added had the industry been located near the source raw materials.

Footloose industries have no locational pull, either to the source of raw materials or to the market. the textile industry is a good example. The cotton industry in Manchester was attracted there by the moisture, which protected cotton thread from breaking. Liverpool held another attraction in that it was where cotton from the USA was unloaded. The oil-refining industry is another example. The three locational patterns it has passed through are the subject matter of this section of this book.

In conclusion, the theory of location states that, under perfect competition, the location of an industry will be established at places where production and transportation costs are at a minimum. However, natural, technical, social, political, and cultural factors should not be ignored. They have much to say in the determination of industrial location.

Locational trends of oil refineries

Location of oil refineries presents an interesting case for the shifts and changes of an industry from one place to another. The availability of crude oil, the technology of production, transport facilities, the techniques of refining, and the size and patterns of demand for oil products are the determining factors in the location of oil refineries. However, sometimes general economic, political and strategic factors are the decisive determining factors.

From this diversity of factors and variables, three locational trends of oil refineries are evident. The first started with the drilling of the first oil well at Titusville, Pennsylvania in 1895. The main characteristic of this first trend was that oil refineries were located close to the oil fields. This trend continued to be the predominant one until just before the Second World War. A second locational trend then took place – the location of oil refineries near the market for oil products. With the rise of nationalism in Asia, Africa and Latin America, a third trend began – the location of oil refineries in countries where neither oil-fields nor sufficient demand for petroleum products exists. However, with the rising power of OPEC, more emphasis is put on oil refineries near the source of oil, which sets a fourth pattern of location similar to the first one.

(a) *The pull of the source (1895-1938)*

Since 1895, the pull of the source has been the main determining factor in the location of oil refineries. The technology of oil production was very low during the second half of the nineteenth century and the oil engineer was unable to drill any deeper than a few hundred feet. Today the oil engineer can go down 35,000 feet. As a consequence, the exploration and discovery of oil was limited to certain areas and oil refineries were located only in those areas where crude oil was discovered.

The technology of refining was also undeveloped. The percentage of waste through the refining process was high. The marketable yield derived from crude oil was usually less than half of the crude. The supply of oil products was so limited that it was unable to create its own demand. Moreover, the cost of production of crude oil was high and the oil firms were not interegrated as they are today. For that reason, transport costs were an important consideration and, consequently, locations of refining plants were pulled toward the source of crude oil. However, during the second locational trend, transport costs had little weight in deciding the location of oil refineries.

Because of the low level of technology of oil production, the techniques of refining, and the nature of the oil firms, western Europe had a very low oil-energy producing capacity in 1938. According to Shell, its share was 4 per cent of the world total while the USA had 70 per cent. The high percentage for the USA was due mainly to the large American demand for oil products. The Middle East and the Caribbean countries accounted for the remaining percentage.[7] However, according to British Petroleum, the world refining capacity was 258 million tons in 1938. The United States share was 155 million tons; the Caribbean and the Middle East countries had 30 million tons; the other parts of the world had 60 million tons.[8] The two sets of figures do not agree exactly but they do serve the purpose of analysis.

(b) *The pull of the market (1938-1965)*

The changing nature of the oil firms has undermined the theoretical base for the location of oil refineries near the oil-fields. The present integrated oil firms own producing wells, tankers, refining plants, and distribution facilities where 'the relationship between production costs and transport costs becomes a matter of merely juggling figures internal to the company concerned which will be under pressure (for tax and other reasons) to distribute its profit-earning capacity in part according to criteria other than strictly economic ones.'[9] This important conviction of the international oil firms and the significant rate reductions for shipping crude oil together with the economies achieved in moving oil products, have their weights in locating oil refineries near the market.

Not all the international oil firms are fully in balance. This means that there is no matching between crude-oil storage and outlet facilities. This condition has led some oil firms to build refineries in newly discovered markets; such action may be taken by both the balanced and unbalanced firms. The firm which lacks crude oil will come to an agreement with another oil firm which has crude available, take from it the amount needed for the new market, and build the refinery to process it. This condition has contributed to the wide distribution of oil refineries near the markets, especially after the Second World War.

However, the most important factors that led to the increasing number of oil refineries near the market in western Europe and Japan had a political, commercial, and strategic nature. After the Second World War, the western European countries suffered from difficulties in their international balance of payments because of the industrial dislocation and the loss of capital held in foreign countries. The European countries had to increase their exports in order to correct the deficits in their balance of payments. This was not an easy task because of the productive disparity in international trade. The USA was the dominant power in international trade and in order to compete with it, Europe had to increase its productivity.

To achieve significant improvement in productivity of the European industry, western Europe was obliged to adopt modern technology. Western Europe became almost completely dependent on oil imports. As a consequence, western Europe discovered that oil imports constituted a significant element of the deficit in its balance of payments. In addition to the growing value of oil imports, western Europe had to pay in dollars for oil products and capital equipment which came from the USA.

Under political pressure because the traditional economic methods could not solve the problems, by devaluation or depreciation, the oil firms were told to build their refineries in western Europe. A clear and direct statement from the OEEC stated that: 'The paramount need to conserve foreign exchange . . . demands . . . the subordination of purely technical oil economics to the balance of payments considerations.'[10] As a matter of fact, that was not only for balance of payments correction but also for encouraging more employment. Refining is more labour intensive than crude production. It takes almost 3.5 times as many man-days to produce a ton of refined products as a ton of crude oil. Socially, refining has tremendous effects from the technological point of view. Social benefits are derived from the training of the labour force and diversification of the economy. Finally, refining is very necessary for the establishment of petrochemical industries which in turn implies that new opportunities are opened for domestic investment which will create further employment.

Strategic and political factors were paramount in the construction of oil refineries in western Europe. The nationalization of the oil industry in Iran in 1951 by Dr Mossadegh, the stoppage of Middle East oil during the Suez War in October 1956, and the Arab-Israeli War of 1967 taught both the oil companies and the European countries an important lesson — not to build and concentrate the oil refineries in the oil-exporting countries.

This had two implications. First, in case of nationalization the oil companies would be able to counteract the decision taken by the oil-producing government and thus freeze it. This counter action might succeed, since almost all the refineries outside the oil-exporting countries are owned by the oil companies or by their subsidiaries and affiliates. Second, if nationalization succeeded, the oil companies would lose crude sources only and not refining facilities as well. This strategic caution is justified by the fact that a big modern refinery has a high capital cost. This is actually what happened during the early 1970s and is still continuing whereby all the oil-exporting countries will own their own oil facilities.

The new techniques applied in refining made it possible for the oil companies to deal with the problem of variations in demand for oil products. The high degree of flexibility of the new techniques saved the oil firms the added cost of searching for new outlets for their products and of transporting them over long distances.

However, all the factors mentioned above cannot override two

121

economic facts. First, large refineries built in the oil-producing countries can supply different markets and not just one national market. They can benefit from economies of scale and reduce unit marketing costs to a low level. Second, refineries in the producing countries do not have to pay for fuel since natural gas is produced in association with crude oil. The negligible cost incurred in this case is for the construction of collecting facilities. If these two facts are important, then one might say that only political, commercial and strategic factors moved the oil refineries from the oil-producing countries to the consuming areas.

(c) *The pull of nationalism*
The third locational trend takes place in the developing countries where the forces of political and economic nationalism have a decisive role in locating oil refineries in areas where neither a sufficient demand nor a source of crude oil exists. As a general rule, an annual capacity of 40,000 barrels per day (2 million tons) is considered to be a minimum quantity at which a reasonably economical refinery can be built. However, most of the refineries of the developing countries have a low capacity due to insufficient demand for oil products, which makes it advisable to import the oil products they need rather than process them in their countries.

Usually it costs two to three times as much to process one barrel of crude oil in a 500,000-ton refinery as it does in a 4,000,000-ton refinery. Some of the refineries in the developing countries have a high capacity but they are always run at less than full capacity because there is not enough local demand (which makes the unit cost high). Also, to export surplus products is considered uneconomical due to high transport costs and high protective tariffs.

The main factors that override all the comparative advantages of importing oil products rather than processing crude oil at home are of an economic and political nature. With the exception of the oil-exporting countries, all the developing countries, as exporters of primary product, suffer from short- and long-run deficits in their balance of payments. Some of the causes are on the supply side, such as drought, bad irrigation systems, and insufficient information about the market. Other factors affecting the demand side are the development of synthetic industries in the industrially developed countries, the role of Engels's law, and the effects of the business cycle. Because of these factors, the developing countries are suffering from deficits in their balance of payments.

To find a way out of some portion of their deficits, the developing countries found solutions in building refineries to save foreign exchange equivalent to the difference between the price of crude oil and the price of oil products. By this policy Brazil was able to save $196 million in 1961. The same applies to Uruguay. It is also true that building refineries will raise the level of employment and has several social benefits as well as costs. In brief, they are following the same line pursued by western Europe after the Second World War. However, there is a difference between the two groups. The advanced countries of western Europe exerted pressure on their own companies to build refineries in western Europe. The developing countries, however, had no oil companies to put the pressure on, but they did have two ways by which they could build their refineries.

The state could step in and construct and operate refineries, as happened in Chile, Uruguay, Brazil, and other developing countries in Asia and Africa. As a matter of fact, the situation of a surplus supply of crude oil during the early 1960s helped the governments of the developing countries to secure crude oil at a lower price. They did not buy crude oil at posted prices but at discounts sometimes equal to 20 per cent of the posted prices. The most dramatic cases of crude surplus existed in 1959 and 1960 whereby posted prices of crude oil declined by 10 per cent and 6 per cent respectively. The price reduction averaged a total of 27 cents per barrel. If this general average reduction is added to the rate of discount, then the developing countries seem to have been in an advantageous position.

However, the developing countries ceased to be in an advantageous position because of the increasing prices of crude oil as a result of the more active role of the oil-exporting countries and worldwide shortage of oil supply. Nevertheless, the problem could be scrutinized through more co-operation between the oil-exporting countries and the developing world. The oil-exporting countries could build and finance oil refineries in the developing countries on the basis of joint-venture activities or on the basis of product exchange such as copper or iron ore for oil, aluminium for gas and oil, and so forth.

The national oil companies of the oil-exporting countries are now more active and more powerful than before and their financial institutions owned individually or collectively, such as the OPEC Fund, will be able to co-operate in the building and financing of oil refineries in the developing world. This trend could remedy two main drawbacks in the building and financing of oil refineries in a developed country.

123

First, a large refinery could be built instead of a small one and therefore create more or better economic operation than building a small refinery. Second, if the market is small then product-export potentials could be achieved by enabling the developing country to export its surplus oil products to neighbouring countries.

Gas utilization

Natural gas is a mixture of hydrocarbon elements such as methane, ethane, propane, butane, hexane, etc., and non-hydrocarbon elements, such as nitrogen, carbon dioxide, hydrogen sulphide and sulphur, as shown in Table 5.1. It is noticeable that methane constitutes the largest

Table 5.1 *A typical gas composition in Kuwait and the other gulf states*

Component	%
Nitrogen	0.30
Carbon Dioxide	7.38
Hydrogen Sulphide	6.69
Methane	50.96
Ethane	18.48
Propane	10.32
N-Butane	2.94
I-Butane	0.89
N-Pentane	0.82
I-Pentane	0.60
C_6-Hydrocarbons	0.43
C_7-Hydrocarbons	0.17
C_8-Hydrocarbons	0.02
	100.00

Source: Y. S. F. Al-Sabah: *The Economics of Gas Utilization in the Arabian Gulf States*, lecture given by the author at St Antony's College, Oxford, p. 1.

element, followed by the ethane and propane components. This mixture of gases is of two kinds. First, there is the non-associated natural gas which is being produced by itself without any crude-oil production connected with its production. Second, there is the associated gas which is being produced in association with crude-oil production.

All the oil wells of the on-shore oil concessions of Kuwait and the Arabian Gulf states are associated gas-producing oil-fields. However, the gas/oil ratios to the Kuwait oil-fields are much less than those of the Latin American countries, North Africa and the other Arab countries' oil-fields. There are many reasons for these differences in the gas/oil ratios. First, is the quality of crude oil being produced. Heavy-crude-oil producing fields tend to have low gas/oil ratios. This is one of the main characteristics of the Kuwaiti oil-fields, in contrast to some of the oil-fields of the other Gulf States, North Africa, Nigeria and Venezuela. The second important factor is the age of the oil-field itself. The older the oil-field is, the higher the gas/oil ratio. Many other factors are attributed to differences of geological structure.

The economic uses of natural gas are less publicized than those of oil. Not only does it perform the same functions as oil but also it is safer and much cleaner. When it is used as fuel its advantages over oil are longer engine life and more efficient performance. It is also more concentrated than oil in that it can be transported and stored in liquid form and used as gas. Because of its high purity, consistency of composition and the absence of ashes and sulphurous elements, natural gas is the best fuel for the steel industry. There are other advantages for the glass industry: it helps achieve consistency of glass composition; it provides easy control of the melting and manufacturing processes and it has no injurious effects on the glass. But what makes natural gas far superior to oil is its chemical-feedstock characteristics, which are: first, it is easy to crack; second, it is easier to treat and purify; finally, it is easier to store.

The distribution of world reserves of natural gas does not follow the same pattern as that of oil because of the existence of pure natural gas or non-associated gas-fields — such as the Sui gas-field in Pakistan — in non-oil-producing countries. the USSR is by far the richest gas country in the world, containing about 33 per cent of world gas reserves. The Middle East is the second largest gas region, embracing about 20 per cent of international gas reserves. The third largest region in gas reserves is North America, with an estimated reserve of about 17 per cent of world total. It is followed by Africa (mainly Algeria) and western Europe, each with about 9 per cent of international gas reserves. Finally, comes the Far East, South America, China and Eastern Europe, with 5 per cent, 4 per cent and 3 per cent respectively, as shown in Table 5.2.

One cannot, however, be precisely sure about the accuracy of the above-mentioned percentages corresponding to the USSR, China and eastern Europe. It is also well known that the non-associated gas-fields of the Middle East are not included in the oil companies' records. In the Middle East in general and in the Arabian Gulf states in particular the

Table 5.2 *Distribution of world gas reserves*

Country/region	%
USSR	33
Middle East	20
North America	17
Africa	9
Western Europe	9
Far East	5
South America	4
China and Eastern Europe	3
	100%

Source: *Ibid*., p. 3.

major oil companies and the independent oil companies were mainly interested in crude-oil production to the extent that once they encountered a gas well they always decided to shut it off and move to the next well looking for oil. Consequently, the oil companies did not keep a record of the gas wells. This irresponsible practice of the oil companies, coupled with the lack of knowledge on the part of the host governments, accounts for the inaccuracy in assessing the gas reserves of the Arabian Gulf states. The oil and gas reserves are always kept as highly confidential information by the oil companies. Neither Kuwait nor Saudi Arabia really knows about their oil and gas reserves. Recently, a highly confidential report was revealed by the United States Senate Sub-committee on Foreign Relations which halved the figure that is publicly accepted for the real resources of Saudi Arabia.

The consumers of natural gas are the industrial countries, as is shown in Table 5.3. The USA is by far the largest consumer of natural gas and the USSR is the second largest. The west European countries and especially the Netherlands, Belgium, the UK and West Germany have, in the past few years, become fairly large consumers of natural gas, because of the recent discoveries of natural-gas fields and their proximity to their markets. However, the modern chemical and petro-chemical industries as known at the present time have developed first and foremost in the USA because of the availability of crude oil and natural gas. If one looks at an input-output table of the US economy, one cannot miss the enormous contribution of the chemical sector to the gross national product – in particular to specific sectors, such as the agricultural and industrial sectors. After the Second World War, the building of oil refineries in western Europe and Japan furnished both the former and the latter with a base for a modern petrochemical

Table 5.3 *Annual world natural gas consumption, (million tonnes oil equivalent)*

Country	Consumption
USA	560.4
Canada	61.1
Rest of Western Hemisphere	48.0
TOTAL OF WESTERN HEMISPHERE	672.5
Belgium and Luxembourg	10.0
Netherlands	32.9
France	17.0
West Germany	32.1
Italy	15.9
United Kingdom	30.8
Spain	1.0
Rest of Western Europe	6.4
TOTAL WESTERN EUROPE	146.1
Japan	5.1
Australia	4.1
USSR	216.6
Eastern Europe	43.5
China	4.4
Rest of Eastern Hemisphere	4.4
TOTAL EASTERN HEMISPHERE	461.8
WORLD	1,134.3

Source: *Ibid.*, p. 5.

industry dependent mainly on refinery products, gases and their derivatives. Again, the role of the chemical sectors and their contributions to economic growth in Europe and Japan over the past thirty years have been impressive. Why, then, did this not happen in the oil-exporting countries such as Kuwait and the rest of the Arabian Gulf states?

There were several factors which hindered the development of petrochemical industries in Kuwait and the Arabian Gulf states. First, there was the dominance of the traditional oil concessions. The oil companies were mainly interested in maximizing crude-oil exports as soon as possible in order to make better use of the oil resources at their disposal. They were also interested in minimizing their investment in the host countries in order to reduce the value of their assets for fear of nationalization. Consequently, the oil companies opted to flare the associated gas rather than use it as a feedstock for a petrochemical industry or to inject it back in to the oil wells on a large scale. Second, because of the dominance of the international oil companies, the chemical companies, both big and small, American and European, were unable to have access to the flared gas of Kuwait and the Arabian Gulf states. The chemical companies were eager to use the gas within their own systems as a feedstock for their petrochemical products. However, their proposals to the governments of Kuwait and the Arabian Gulf states were completely barred by the political influence of the major oil companies in the Gulf region. Consequently, neither Kuwait nor any of the other Arabian Gulf states used the resources of their natural gas rationally.

However, over the past ten years, several fertilizer plants have been constructed in Kuwait and the Gulf states, using natural gas as their feedstock to produce ammonia and urea. At the same time, several liquefied petroleum gas plants were erected to produce butane and propane for the export market. Apart from this, which only used a very minute percentage, natural gas was used to produce electricity and desalinated water. In the early years of the 1970s and with the increase in oil and gas prices, coupled with a general awareness about the chemical and fuel importance of natural gas, Kuwait and the rest of the oil-producing countries in the Middle East started thinking seriously about the utilization of their flared gas. As far as an economic gas policy is concerned there are three routes which could be followed.

Conservation

First, there is conservation. Since almost all the production of natural gas in Kuwait and the Arabian Gulf states is associated gas then a policy of oil conservation applies to gas production as well. However, if natural gas is to be conserved and protected for future use then it has to be injected back into the oil wells. Gas injection, however, implies capital investment in collecting and pressurizing facilities, and the oil companies were reluctant to make this investment. Apart from conservation, gas injection helps keep pressure maintenance and prevent future physical waste of oil and gas resources.

As mentioned earlier, a conservation policy was imposed in Kuwait by parliamentary legislation. Kuwait has set an example for the other Arabian Gulf states to follow. Iraq, however, may not follow the same policy. The main reason is that Iraq is in need of a substantial amount of capital to finance its huge agricultural and industrial projects. Therefore it discounts its future income from oil and gas at a lower rate than the other capital-surplus countries such as Kuwait and the rest of the Arabian Gulf states. There is no doubt that Saudi Arabia and the other smaller Arabian Gulf states will, under mounting public pressure, follow a reasonable and long-lasting conservation policy in the near future. The international consequences of such a policy are beyond the subject matter of this book.

Industry

Second, the alternative to conservation is the use of natural gas as a fuel for industry and agriculture. There are certain industries which are capital and energy intensive, such as aluminium, copper, steel, glass, ceramics, magnesium oxide, etc. The aluminium industry in Bahrain proved to be a successful one. Aluminium is imported from Australia by oil/bulk/ore tankers. However, instead of going back empty, the vessels carry crude oil from ports of the Arabian Gulf states. This kind of transport logistics reduces the cost of the raw material needed to feed the plant in Bahrain. This kind of joint venture proved the importance of the roles played by the host government and the foreign partner. The former provides the project with assured continuous supply of natural gas at a reasonable price and the ability to borrow money; the latter provides the project with raw material based on long-term supply, technology, marketing capabilities and know-how. The combination of both roles helped Bahrain to build a basic industry out of which other chains of the same industry could be established (such as aluminium extrusion and rolling plants). The finished products enjoy the growth markets of the Middle East.

Likewise, the availability of raw copper in the Sultanate of Oman could utilize the flared gases in order to establish another basic industry in the Gulf region. The market for copper already exists in the Middle East. There are several plants which make copper bars and wires but depend on foreign supplies for their input. The making of copper foil uses a large amount of natural gas. It is widely used in the building industry as a moisture barrier and it is also used in the making of electrical circuits.

The glass industry is another possible investment area: this could be established in Kuwait using imported sand, since the Kuwaiti sand is not suitable for glass-making. As a rule of thumb, more than 35 per cent of the cost of production of glass is attributed to fuel. In making glass, natural gas has the following advantages. First, it assures the consistency of glass composition. Second, by using natural gas it is easier to control the melting and manufacturing processes. Third, because of its purity, the manufacturers can be absolutely certain that no contaminating substance is present in the worked glassware. The other elements of cost are sand and capital, which could be obtained from neighbouring countries and Kuwait respectively. The market for glass products in the Middle East is growing at a high rate due to the predicted growth of the building and construction industry. Thousands of new schools and houses and several hospitals are going to be built over the coming five years, in addition to private residential and commercial buildings. The only missing factors are technology and management which could easily be provided by potential foreign partners.

Magnesium oxide is another important industry which is based directly and indirectly on natural gas: directly because it uses gas as fuel, and indirectly because it uses brine, a by-product of water desalination, as its input. Kuwait has several desalination plants which produce water, caustic soda, chlorine and brine. Brine is presently available in Kuwait at a rate of more than 62 million gallons per day. Its chemical composition is as follows:

Chlorine	28740	MG/kg
Sodium	15841	MG/kg
Magnesium	1908	MG/kg
Calcium	600	MG/kg
Potassium	570	MG/kg
Specific gravity	1.049	MG/kg

From the above chemical composition of brine, together with the availability of cheap fuel based on natural gas and low-cost capital, Kuwait could easily build a plant that could produce 500 tons a day of magnesium oxide. To indicate how profitable such a project would be, suffice it to say that the cost per ton in Kuwait does not exceed US $340 while the f.o.b. price is more than US $500.

Magnesium oxide is used to produce magnesium metal, which is used to make refractories in the form of bricks and cement. It is also widely used by the chemical industry, especially by the rubber and tyre industries.

Despite the opportunities available for the use of natural gas to diversify the economy, there has been no attempt to exploit them. They are not labour-intensive projects in conflict with government policy. On the contrary, they are capital-intensive industries which could utilize Kuwaiti capital that is at present being eroded in value in the vaults of the international commercial banks as a result of rising inflation.

Kuwait has not to date exploited its location and the wide opportunities that would be created by a transport logistics system. Even the Kuwaiti and the Arab Peninsula deserts could bloom through an appropriate transport logistics system based on oil exports. The west European countries have plentiful supplies of peat but are thirsty for oil. A project could utilize the present tanker-system routes to export crude oil from Kuwait to, for example, the largest oil terminal in Europe (mainly in Bantry Bay). However, instead of oil tankers returning empty, a load of peat could enjoy free, or nearly free, transport to Kuwait. The objective would be to cover the desert with peat so that the desert would be able to retain water. If this could happen, then several opportunities would be available in the agricultural field for capital and labour; or at least, in the case of an international crisis it would still be possible to secure one's loaf of bread.

Petrochemicals

The third obvious route open to Kuwait and the other Arabian Gulf gas-flaring countries is the utilization of natural gas to produce basic and intermediate petrochemical products such as ammonia, urea, ethylene, propylene, butadiene and isoprene. These basic products are the necessary inputs for the production of a large number of various and intermediate and final products, as shown.

Ethylene derivatives
  1 Low-density polyethylene
  2 High-density polyethylene
  3 Ethylene-propylene rubber
  4 Ethylene oxide
  5 Ethylene glycol
  6 Ethylbenzene and styrene
  7 Ethylene dichloride, vinyl chloride and PVC
  8 Ethanol
  9 Acetic acid
 10 Vinyl acetate
 11 Alpha-olepins
 12 Linear alcohols

Propylene derivatives
  1 Polypropylene
  2 Ethylene-propylene rubber

3 Cumene for phenol and acetone
4 Propylene oxide
5 Propylene glycol
6 Acrylonitrile
7 Acrylic acid
8 Isopropanol
9 Isoprene
10 Oxoalcohols
11 Butyraldehydes
12 Propylene trimer and tetramaer

Butadiene derivatives
1 SBR rubber
2 Styrene butadiene acrylonitrile terpolymer
3 Nitrile rubber
4 Polybutadiene rubber
5 Propellants
6 Adiponitrile and Heamthylenediamine

Isoprene derivatives
1 Butyl rubber
2 Polyisoprene rubber

Most of the above-mentioned products could be produced in Kuwait more cheaply than elsewhere because of certain comparative cost advantages that Kuwait possesses. First, Kuwait is able to build very large petrochemical plants in order to maximize the benefits inherent in the economics of large-scale production. It is a well-known fact in business economics that doubling the capacity of the plant does not mean doubling the costs of it. The yardstick that is generally used is 40 per cent savings as a result of doubling the capacity of the plant. Second, Kuwait possesses cheap raw materials to feed the plant and cheap fuel to run it. Third, is the availability in Kuwait of capital at a low rate of interest. This is especially important since the capital needed to build a large petrochemical complex exceeds a billion dollars.

However, several problems lie ahead, such as co-ordination among the Arabian Gulf gas-flaring countries in order to avoid cut-throat competition in the production and marketing of petrochemicals. It goes without saying that there will be enormous managerial, industrial and marketing problems, which will necessitate the role of the foreign partner because of his industrial marketing know-how. It goes without saying, also, that downstream investments are capital intensive with a high degree of risk emanating from changing technology, and that therefore the price of failure is very high. Success in downstream operations depends on the availability of a high level of material and human infrastructure. Finally, the political problems that will undoubtedly arise as a result of rapid industrialization in a traditional society are not to be discounted. However, most Arab intellectuals are prepared to accept these political problems, since their early solution is considered to be the first step towards a mature, developed society.

Downstream investments and their obstacles

Although the member countries of OPEC accounted for more than 87 per cent of world oil exports, their share of world refinery capacity was around 6 per cent in 1978. Even if all the planned oil refineries in the member countries of OPEC implemented their share in world refinery capacity, it would not exceed 9 per cent by 1981. The same applies to the execution of the planned petrochemical projects in OPEC member countries, which will not exceed 13 per cent of the petrochemical capacity of the free world by 1981. It is this kind of situation which the member countries of OPEC find so unacceptable and which will leave them basically as suppliers of raw material for quite a long time to come. Their anger and frustration are based on the following facts:

(i) the capital-deficit countries of OPEC are plagued with problems of unemployment, deficits in their international balances of payment and low indices of social and economic development;

(ii) they are endowed with highly valued natural resources from which they cannot derive the value added to finished and semi-finished products derived from these resources;

(iii) these resources are exhaustible in the very near future;

(iv) industrializing the oil and gas sector will inject into their own country supply-and-demand linkages which will lead to an overall industrialization and a higher rate of economic growth;

(v) if these countries are unable to industrialize *now* they will miss their opportunities for ever.

However, among some member countries of OPEC, there is concern that their industrialization plans are not proceeding as quickly as they hoped. They have been unable to finance their projects and to obtain the technology at a reasonable price from the highly developed countries.

Their problems were compounded by administrative and tax barriers to their products in the consuming countries, and were exacerbated further by the shortage of indigenous managerial ability to run their plants in the absence of foreign partners demanding various high-valued concessions from the host countries.

The management of the oil sector

Compared with the large and medium-size member countries of OPEC, Kuwait is a small country. However, its role in OPEC is a reflection of its greater capacity to produce oil per day and its reserves. It uses a higher percentage of its flared gas than any other member of the Organization of Arab Petroleum-Exporting Countries (OAPEC). At the same time, it refines more oil, in percentage terms, than the rest of the Gulf states. Nevertheless, Kuwait's policies towards downstream operations are not clearly defined and lack a central planning power geared to a welldefined objective.

Kuwait now has full control of its oil resources. The oil sector is composed of the Ministry of Oil, Kuwait Oil Company (KOC), Kuwait National Petroleum Company (KNPC) and Petrochemical Industries Company (PIC). The Ministry of Oil has developed from a Department for Oil Affairs within the Ministry of Finance to a joint ministry as the Ministry of Oil and Finance. Until it becomes a fully fledged ministry with a single cabinet status it will mainly be concerned with the overall supervision of the oil sector and the marketing of crude oil.

The other components of the oil sector are KOC, KNPC, and PIC. Each company has its own budget-making authority and follows its independent policy with regard to oil and gas in downstream operations. Each company naturally also wishes to secure a leading role in the oil sector. In practice, however, this can lead to an emphasis on competition between the companies rather than upon a national policy for the utilization of gas and oil.

There is still no guidance forthcoming as to the percentage of crude oil to be refined locally. Both KOC and KNPC have several plans for refining higher percentages of crude oil than at present. However, the two companies have different ideas as to the products they should produce and the market they should satisfy. Guidance over this issue would remove a major obstacle from the oil sector.

At the present time KOC is operating an oil refinery similar to those built in Europe a quarter of a century ago. More than 52 per cent of its product is composed of high-sulphur heavy fuel oil which has a market value below that of the crude oil that is used as its input. KOC has a plan to add a desulphurizator unit to its refinery in order to upgrade its product; however, this kind of upgrading would not add more than 15 per cent to the value of its product, which would continue to sell below the value of its input.

The Ministry of Oil must take full control of economic activity and future planning regarding the building of oil refineries and petrochemical plants, to ensure that oil and gas resources and their downstream operations are managed in the best possible way.

Restrictions on foreign investment

The Kuwaiti commercial laws are derived from Egyptian, Syrian, Lebanese and Iraqi commercial codes. All these sister Arab countries are underdeveloped and almost all of them suffer at different times from balance-of-payments deficits and unemployment. To apply the same laws in Kuwait seems inadvisable, because Kuwait enjoys a unique position. It is a very small country and its domestic market does not suffer from either unemployment or balance-of-payments deficits. In point of fact, Kuwait suffers from capital surplus on three fronts: its national savings exceed its domestic investment; its public revenue exceeds its public expenditure; and its balance of payments has always been an overall surplus.

The role of foreign investment is multiple, provided it is well directed. It brings technology, know-how and entrepreneurial skills. It contributes to national income through payments to local factors of production. It contributes to the public budget through taxes. Finally, it has a growth effect by injecting forward and backward linkages into the economy, which ultimately leads to changes in the structure of the economy. It is this last point which is of far-reaching importance for Kuwait. Chapter 4 revealed the dualistic nature of the Kuwaiti economy between the oil sector and the non-oil sector. Chapter 3 demonstrated the role of foreign investment in its application to the development of the oil resources of Kuwait, its contribution to the national budget and to social and economic development. The question is: Why are foreign chemical companies not investing in Kuwait in order to inject the growth-generating effect into the oil sector itself? In the past the hegemony of the old oil concessions prevented this. At the present time, however, it appears to be a question of management problems within the oil sector. Joint ventures with well-established firms in oil and petrochemicals would surely help in the marketing and management of petrochemical products.

The present law of commercial companies requires that the proportion of Kuwaiti capital in any commercial enterprise must not be less than 51 per cent. For the sake of the economic growth it would generate, the 49 per cent limit on foreign companies could be raised to 85 per cent in favour of the foreign companies for certain industries. Subsidies could also be made available to encourage certain foreign firms in Kuwait — for example, pharmaceutical companies. Kuwait could be a good location for such companies who want entry into the Arab market of the Middle East. Such policies should be viewed in terms of the industrial future of Kuwait after the oil era.

Shipping companies should be encouraged through subsidies and tax exemption until they have a strong foothold in Kuwait. The time is now ripe for this step, while shipping companies can be bought by Kuwaiti businessmen at low prices. In other words, international opportunities should be sought while a large capital surplus is available (which is being eroded every day by world inflation and dollar depreciation) and investment in the future likelihood of certain industries and services in Kuwait should be made. The examples are numerous. However, what is needed is a flexibility in the commercial laws of Kuwait and future planning to take advantage of the current low prices but with future higher values for Kuwait. This kind of policy could cover a wide range of industries, including banking, insurance, transport and other scientific-base companies.

Labour and the law of naturalization

In previous chapters, it was demonstrated that the government played a significant role in social and economic development. However, in the 1960s, with the growth of new elites and interest groups, the new economic policies adopted by the government, reflected in its commercial and labour laws, had certain effects which now prevent change in the structure of the economy and in particular within the labour force.

Economic development in Kuwait has introduced new problems and complexities by increasing the importance of the role of capital and labour. These complexities have not weakened the power of the political system, because of the adoption of a parliamentary system of government. However, after the dissolution of parliament on 29 August 1976, the government began to face serious problems as a result of rapid economic development and its consequences. Although the merchant upper class and the new middle class gained political power through parliament and the press, nevertheless the government limited the impact of immigration by adopting certain laws that reduced the effectiveness of the role of foreign labour in general and of the foreign entrepreneur in particular.

The fact that non-Kuwaitis are not integrated in the host country means that they are not accommodated in a way that could eventually lead to their assimilation. If the future assimilation of the non-Kuwaitis is not taken seriously into account, this will mean a great economic waste. It is true that assimilation is a lengthy process but it is also equally true that certain changes in the social and institutional structures are necessary to expedite the absorption of immigrants. Although the influx of immigrants into Kuwait has been increasing since 1946, nevertheless the government has restricted them to the classification of temporary visitors through its law of naturalization. It should be stated that these were the wishes of a large number of members of parliament since the establishment of the parliamentary system in Kuwait. The first article of the Law of Naturalization states that:[11]

The Kuwaitis are those who lived in Kuwait before the year 1920

This article clearly prevents immigrants from becoming Kuwaiti nationals simply because immigrants did not start to come to Kuwait in large numbers until after the discovery of oil in 1946. Article Four of the same law, which is less restrictive than Article One, states that:[12]

Nationality could be given to any person who lived in Kuwait for fifteen successive years on the condition that he entered Kuwait by legal ways, speaks the Arabic language, and his profession is in need in Kuwait.

However, the spirit of the law of naturalization is even more restrictive than the articles defining its rules and regulations. It is also not difficult to predict the social, political and economic consequences of that law. The law implies that immigrants will remain temporarily in Kuwait for work and that they could be deported if the government did not renew the contracts of skilled personnel or issue identity cards for unskilled labourers. Kuwait is not alone in such regards: West Germany,

Switzerland and other western European countries have even more restrictive regulations concerning foreign labour.

What complicates the problem in Kuwait is that because the immigrants come from different Arab and non-Arab countries it is felt that they could not organize themselves in one social group. However:[13]

> When a certain number of individuals in the midst of a political society are found to have ideas, interests, sentiments and occupations not shared by the rest of the population, it is inevitable that they will be attracted toward each other under the influence of these likenesses. They will seek each other out, enter into relations, associate and thus little by little, a restricted group, having its social characteristics, will be formed in the midst of the general society.

It is a *prima facie* objective that political stability must be seen as a necessary condition for economic progress. A sense of community cannot be developed under the present restrictive laws. A sense of continuity and assurance will help the immigrants to establish and expand their businesses. These conditions are important for potential successful businessmen and provide a challenge for Kuwaitis to enter various fields of productive economic activity rather than to remain mostly dependent on the government.

(1) Labour-force occupational participation rates

The demographic structure of Kuwait shows an interesting but challenging fact that is not to be found in any other part of the world. The fact is that the Kuwaiti element as a percentage of the total population has been decreasing since 1946. The general population census of 1957 recorded the percentage of Kuwaitis in the total population as 55 per cent. However, in 1961 the non-Kuwaiti element surpassed the Kuwaiti by 0.4 per cent. By 1965 the non-Kuwaiti percentage in the total population reached 3 per cent above that of the Kuwaiti population. The population census of 1975 indicated that the non-Kuwaiti element continued to exceed by far the percentage of Kuwaitis in the total population (by about 2.5 per cent). No other country would permit such a situation to occur, yet no action has been taken to correct the demographic picture of Kuwait or at least to minimize this danger.

The participation rates of Kuwaitis and non-Kuwaitis in the labour force reveal an even more startling picture. According to the 1965 population census, Kuwaitis accounted for 23 per cent of the labour force, while non-Kuwaitis accounted for 77 per cent. These figures reached their most extreme in January 1969, at 18 per cent and 82 per cent respectively. By 1975, the participation rate of the Kuwaitis had increased to 30 per cent. This was the result of an increasing number of naturalized Kuwaitis, but consisting mainly of unskilled Bedouin labour rather than skilled doctors, engineers, etc.

The distribution of the labour force among various economic activities is shown in Table 5.4, which shows the predominance of non-Kuwaitis in all kinds of economic activity. The services sector enjoys the highest number of non-Kuwaitis in the labour force. The wholesale and retail trade section is the second highest economic activity in which the non-Kuwaitis number more than the Kuwaitis themselves. Since 1957 the number of non-Kuwaitis in all kinds of economic activity has been increasing and some sectors of the economy have been increasingly dominated by them. This is partly because of the unwillingness of Kuwaitis to enter certain kinds of economic activity and partly because of their lack of professional experience and qualifications for such economic activity, a fact that is supported by the better educational status of the foreign elements of the labour force in comparison with the Kuwaiti element.

(2) Manpower projection

In the present century almost every nation is concerned with manpower development to the extent that a new branch of economic science is evolving which goes far beyond traditional labour economics. Because of the novelty of the field, there are many unsolved problems and difficulties concerning the type of forecast needed and methodological techniques employed. In general, manpower projection can deal either with needs or with probable demand in the economy. In view of the special nature of the labour force in Kuwait, manpower projection in this book will try to answer the following questions: What will be the volume of the labour force in 1990? What will be the number of non-Kuwaitis in the labour force in 1990? Given an annual increase of 1 per cent in the participation rate of non-Kuwaitis in the labour force, what then will be their rate of participation in 1990? What adaptations are needed in the nature of the law of naturalization if the same rate of economic growth and political stability are to be maintained?

Table 5.4 Labour force by division of economic activity in census years 1957, 1965, 1970, 1975

Sections of economic activity	Sex	Census 1975*		Census 1970		Census 1965		Census 1957	
Agriculture, hunting and fishing	M	3,522	3,970	3,253	798	1,408	666	446	603
	F	9	13	5	4	2	7	–	–
Mining and quarrying	M	2,953	1,767	4,828	1,627	5,241	1,337	4,088	1,211
	F	127	12	668	48	402	12	106	–
Manufacturing industries	M	21,889	2,237	25,876	6,100	16,103	1,823	5,539	1,009
	F	320	21	106	9	14	2	43	20
Construction	M	30,357	1,755	31,418	2,186	27,566	1,262	8,025	378
	F	143	1	66	2	18	2	–	–
Electricity, gas and water	M	5,230	2,029	5,106	2,130	5,341	1,645	–	–
	F	7	5	13	3	5	–	–	–
Wholesale and retail trade	M	32,364	6,297	25,181	7,261	17,769	5,115	4,058	4,107
	F	868	30	534	37	147	14	15	44
Transportation and communication	M	10,853	4,305	9,640	2,357	7,336	2,612	2,053	1,513
	F	265	262	136	5	76	1	–	–
Services	M	76,751	57,306	54,401	34,919	50,123	24,571	27,697	14,365
	F	25,786	6,959	12,909	1,907	6,892	948	1,522	316
Activities not adequately defined	M	–	–	559	236	611	232	3,583	4,803
	F	–	2	21	5	64	17	7	4

TOTAL ACTIVITY									
	M	183,919	79,666	160,262	57,614	131,498	39,163	55,489	27,989
	F	27,525	7,305	14,458	2,020	7,620	1,003	1,693	384
	T	211,444	86,971	174,720	59,634	139,118	40,166	57,182	28,373
Inactive	M	17,206	38,863	17,341	43,123	10,240	25,583	6,180	10,472
	F	86,634	112,812	68,938	96,894	35,580	60,772	10,430	34,903
TOTAL POPULATION	M	201,125	118,529	177,603	100,737	141,738	64,746	61,669	38,461
	F	114,159	120,117	83,396	98,914	43,200	61,775	12,123	35,287
	T	315,284	238,646	260,999	199,651	184,938	126,521	73,792	73,748

* Population in census 1975 (15 years and over).

Source: Central Statistical Office, Annual Statistical Abstract, Ministry of Planning, 1977, Kuwait, p. 86.

Methodology

The Harrod-Demar model is used here to forecast manpower requirements. In this model the growth rates of labour and capital are projected by the use of two independent production functions as follows:

$$Y = a' + K'K$$
$$Y = b'N$$

where

a' = constant
K' = the marginal output-capital ratio
b' = the marginal output-labour ratio
K = quantity of capital used to produce a given level of output
N = quantity of labour used to produce a given level of output

Then from these two production functions, the growth rate of output is arrived at as follows:

$$\frac{dy}{Y} = K'\frac{dK}{Y}$$

$$\frac{dY}{Y} = b'\frac{dN}{Y}$$

However, this book is concerned only with the projection of manpower requirements. This could be arrived at by getting the output-labour ratio, b', and labour policy. Then, by the year 1990, the whole volume of the labour force in Kuwait will be foreign. Again, if ones assumes that the Kuwaiti elements in the labour force will increase by 2 per cent every year, which is unlikely, then in 1990 the foreign-labour participation rate will continue to be as high as 42 per cent.

These results seriously question the population policy and the educational system in Kuwait. After thirty-five years of systematic education, the Kuwaiti educational system is not producing the skilled manpower the country needs. The question is: What are the alternative policies before the government to maintain political stability and economic growth? Without any change in the law of naturalization and the natural limit of population growth, the present educational system will not be able to produce enough manpower to replace the non-Kuwaiti elements in the labour force.

If any change in the law of naturalization is made without improvement in educational policy towards the Kuwaitis, there will be serious political conflict in the future between the old Kuwaitis and the newly naturalized Kuwaitis. This is because the new Kuwaitis will not be treated on an equal basis with the old Kuwaitis. The only way out of these problems is to move on two fronts: first, the law of naturalization must be liberalized gradually; and, second, the educational system must be changed to match the envisaged structural change in the economy.

Chapter 6

The changing price structure of crude oil

This chapter will trace the development of crude-oil prices from the two major oil-export areas — the Gulf of Mexico and the the Arabian Gulf — and analyse the factors behind the decrease or increase in the price of crude oil from the Second World War to the present time. The reason for choosing this period is that after the Second World War there was more international trade in crude oil because of the shift of oil refineries from the producing countries to the consuming countries of Europe and Japan.

Gulf of Mexico-plus formula

Most of the world demand for oil was supplied by the USA and Mexico, the leading exporters of petroleum before the Second World War. The international price of crude oil was based on the Gulf of Mexico formula. This formula simply meant that all buyers of crude oil anywhere in the world should pay United States Gulf price plus freight from the Gulf to its destination, regardless of the availability of oil at a lower cost per barrel from another oil-field. This kind of pricing system increased the rate of return of the oil companies in general and the international oil companies in the Middle East in particular, because they had a transport-cost advantage for delivery to the eastern Mediterranean area.

Before the Second World War, the supply of oil was characterized by three main aspects:[1]

(i) The United States oil industry was by far the largest in the world.

(ii) United States exports from the Gulf Coast covered a large part of the world's demand, with other western Hemisphere and Middle East supplies still in the process of rapid expansion and development.

(iii) The United States Gulf was practically the only place where importers could obtain supplies and spot cargoes on the open market to cover any likely requirements.

However, the Gulf of Mexico price was not justified by the fact that the USA was the great supplier of oil. The oil industry since its inception has never been exposed to a really competitive market. Federal Trade Commission Staff Reports stated that Gulf-plus pricing was a result of conservation policy. The United States crude-oil prices were regulated by the Texas Railroad Commission. In 1930, the Supreme Court ruled that the commission had the power to fix production for each field and well. Prices were high enough to cover the costs of the United States marginal oil producers. Thus, the small producers were protected, while the international major producers received exorbitant profits. This cartel agreement worked well but not completely without trouble. The small independent companies continued to export their oil at prices lower than those of the cartel members.

A new basing-point[2]

During and after the Second World War huge deposits of oil were discovered in the Middle East. This discovery coincided with the economic recovery of Europe, brought about in large part by the Marshall Plan. As a result of this change, the conventional international price of oil underwent a structural change. The Arabian Gulf became a basing-point in determining the price of crude oil. This was not a minor change. The Arabian Gulf f.o.b. prices were lowered by an amount equal to the cost of transport from the United States Gulf Coast to the Arabian Gulf – approximately $2.95 per barrel to $1.05 per barrel. By 1946, the USA removed price controls and consequently the price of crude oil in the United States Gulf began to increase until it reached its maximum point in December 1947 – $1.46 per barrel above the wartime price, of $4.41 per barrel. The Arabian Gulf crude prices followed suit, but by a lesser amount than United States Gulf prices. The increase was only $1.17 per barrel above wartime price, of $2.25 per barrel.

In May 1948, while the US price of crude oil remained constant, the Arabian Gulf prices began to decline. The decline was $0.47 per barrel, and the price of the Arabian Gulf oil became $0.76 lower than the price of US Gulf crude. However, prices of Arabian Gulf crude were reduced further. In April 1949, Middle East prices went down $0.15 and in July of the same year a further reduction of $0.13 took place.

Basically there are two main factors behind the reduction of crude-oil prices on the Arabian Gulf. First, the Economic Cooperation Administration exerted great pressure on the oil companies to reduce the price of crude oil and products of the Middle East to finance Europe with cheap oil. The ECA was adopting the formula of Dr P. H. Frankel who had suggested that the f.o.b. price of Arabian Gulf crude oil be equal to the US Gulf Coast price plus the cost of freight from the nearest source of supply. This formula was planned to eliminate geographical price discrimination against Europe. The ECA was also encouraged by the latest estimates of proved reserves in the Middle East. The US commission which surveyed the oil resources of the Middle East in 1944 found the estimated proved reserves to be 18 billion barrels instead of previous estimates of 5 billion barrels. The new estimates at that time raised the Middle East percentage of world total reserves from 17 per cent to 37 per cent.

The second main factor behind the price reduction of Arabian Gulf crude oil lies in the nature of the international integrated oil companies. The ECA succeeded, through its pressure on the oil companies, in reducing the price of crude oil from the Arabian Gulf. However, it failed to accomplish a reduction in the price of oil products. Its success, in fact, coincided with the wishes of the integrated oil companies to reduce the price of crude oil because this would increase their profits from refining and distributing operations.[3]

> For an integrated company, the price at which crude oil is transferred from producing to refining affiliates determines the distribution of its total profit between crude production and refining. For any given level and structure of product prices and costs, the higher the transfer price of crude oil, the lower the profits attributed to refining and distribution, but total profits are unaffected by the internal (accounting) distribution of profits.

These were the main reasons which led to a reduction in the price of crude oil. The element of competition could not be used to explain the price reduction at that time, for there was no competition at all in determining the price of crude oil. However, competition would come later through the influence of the independent oil companies and the nature of the imbalance of the international integrated oil companies.

The Korean War and after

After the Korean War, the price of crude oil began to increase in both the United States Gulf Coast and the Arabian Gulf. However, the price increases were not identical in the two areas: 30 cents in the United States Gulf Coast as against 10 cents in the Arabian Gulf. Both prices were for the same API gravity of crude oil (34°). Phillips Petroleum Company, which is a fully integrated company, but without interest in the Middle East at the time, initiated the price increase. It was followed by the American and Venezuelan producers. Later on, producers in the Middle East announced their price increase. The explanation for the price increase in the USA was based on three factors. First, there was a sharp increase in exploration and production costs. Second, there was the need to maintain a large excess producing capacity for defence purposes. Third, there was the need for internal financing because of the difficulty in raising capital from the market to cover costs of exploration and production.

The question of pricing crude oil

The price problem was raised between the exporting countries and the producing companies when the latter, without previous consultation with the exporting countries, initiated another two rounds of price reduction. The first was in February 1959, which amounted to 10 per cent off the posted price. The second reduction took place in August 1960, and amounted to 6 per cent off the posted price. These two decreases averaged $0.27 per barrel. The reductions in crude-oil prices affected only the Middle East and Venezuela. There was no decline in prices in the US Gulf Coast.

It was oligopolistic competition that forced reductions in the posted prices on which payments to the exporting governments are based. As a matter of fact, not all the major internationals were in balance. Probably only Esso was in equilibrium, while Shell and Mobil were short of cheap crudes. On the other hand, BP, CFP and Gulf had surpluses of crude oil which were unmatched by their controlled outlets. It was BP, CFP and Gulf who first started to give a lower posted price in order to be able to market their surpluses. The non-integrated independent oil companies also cut prices of crude oil. By offering low prices to independent refiners, the major internationals were subsidising their competition on a large scale. This process caused the marketing affiliates of the integrated companies to cut their prices. Probably Soviet oil had an impact on the oil market which, with the competition of the independent oil companies and the nature of imbalance among the major internationals, led to price reductions in 1959 and 1960. However, the prime motivation behind the beginning of the reductions in posted price was:[4]

> If it made sense to take the host governments in as sleeping partners with half share in an extraordinary margin, it was also plain good business to give away part of what was left, in order to be able to make better use of oil reserves at one's disposal or, in extremis, to retain one's concession.

The second reduction in the posted price of crude oil in the Middle East and Venezuela (put into effect in August 1960) was strongly opposed by the host governments. As a reaction to price reduction, the five major petroleum-exporting countries (Iran, Iraq, Kuwait, Saudi Arabia and Venezuela) called for a conference in Baghdad in September 1960. The conference decided to establish the Organization of Petroleum Exporting Countries (OPEC). Qatar joined the organization in January 1961, Libya and Indonesia followed suit in June 1962, Abu Dhabi in 1967, Algeria in 1969, Nigeria in 1971, Ecuador in 1973 and Gabon in 1975.

All the member countries have similar features. All of them are underdeveloped countries and net exporters of crude oil. Almost all of their oil resources are under the control of the seven international oil companies. They realized that they could not individually force the solid oligopolistic power of the oil companies. The only way out was a collective organization with the power to control the supply of crude oil. However, it must be remembered that the idea of a petroleum organization had its roots among some of the Arab countries who were desirous of protecting their interests. That desire among the Arab members was assisted by the fear of Venezuela that Arab crude oil was showing an economic advantage over Latin American crude. During the first Arab petroleum congress in Cairo in 1959, the real discussion started between the Arab member countries and non-Arab oil delegates, which resulted in a gentleman's agreement regarding the establishment of OPEC.

At the fourth conference of OPEC (held in Geneva in 1963) three important claims were raised against the oil companies. The first called for the restoration of posted prices of crude oil in the Middle East to the levels prevailing before August 1960. The second called for an end to the marketing allowance which the oil companies offer to their affiliates and subsidiaries. The third claim called for the expensing of royalties, that is to say, to treat royalties as expense before the payment of the 50 per cent income tax. This last claim was accepted by the oil companies on the condition that they would be given an allowance of discount equal to 8.5 per cent of the posted price for the first year of agreement, 1964, and 7.5 per cent and 6.5 per cent for the years 1965 and 1966 respectively. However, the first claim, which called for the restoration of prices prevailing before August 1960, was not accepted until ten years later.

As a matter of fact it was only in the 1970s that OPEC began to gather strength as far as crude-oil prices are concerned. The main reason for the increase in crude-oil prices could be attributed first to the strategic move of the Libyan Government. In August 1970 the Libyan Government refused to negotiate with the oil companies collectively and asked for individual company negotiation. It started with Occidental and forced the latter to increase the posted price of Libyan crude oil by 30 cents. After that the Libyan Government turned round against the other oil companies and threatened to stop oil exports from Libya if they did not increase the Libyan posted price. The oil companies could not resist the Libyan demands for long and thus the increase in crude-oil prices spread to cover all member countries of OPEC.

It must be mentioned at this point that the strategic move of Libya was significantly strengthened by, first, the closure of the Suez Canal, second, the disruption of Tapline and, third, by the increase in demand for oil in western Europe and Japan. All these factors led the Arabian Gulf states to increase tax rates from 50 per cent to 55 per cent and to increase crude-oil prices for heavy crudes by 9 cents per barrel.

The scene of the battle between the oil companies and the oil-exporting countries shifted to Venezuela, which legislated unilaterally by increasing tax from 52 per cent to 60 per cent. In Venezuela the OPEC conference (held 8-12 December 1970) asked for the following:

(i) A 55 per cent minimum tax rate.
(ii) Elimination of existing disparities in tax prices after taking into account gravity, location and escalation in future years.
(iii) A uniform general increase in crude-oil prices to reflect supply-and-demand conditions.
(iv) A new gravity formula based upon 15 cents per $0.1°$
(v) Elimination of all allowance for tax purposes.

On 2 January 1971, Libya jumped the gun and demanded individual company negotiations; however, it was unsuccessful because of the lack of co-operation from other members of OPEC.

The events in Venezuela led to negotiations in Iran which terminated in the Tehran agreement of 14 February 1971. The main points of the Tehran agreement were as follows:

(i) The agreement is effective 15 February 1971 and runs for five years to 31 December 1975.
(ii) During the agreement the Gulf states shall not take any action in the Gulf (restrict or shut down production) to support any OPEC member making demands above these agreed terms.
(iii) During this agreement no Gulf state will seek any increased government take or other financial obligations over that now agreed, as a result of the application of different terms under various circumstances.
(iv) The five points contained in OPEC resolution XXI-120 adopted at Caracas in December 1970 are met by the following financial terms:
  (a) the present tax laws lower than 55 per cent will be adjusted to that level;
  (b) a 33 cents per barrel general increase in posted prices on all Persian Gulf crudes;
  (c) an inflation factor of 2.5 per cent of new posted prices to take effect 1 June 1971 and thereafter on 1 January 1973, 1974 and 1975;
  (d) a further inflation factor of 5 cents per barrel increase in posted prices effective 1 June 1971 and thereafter on 1 January 1973, 1974 and 1975;
  (e) 2 cents per barrel increase in posted prices on all crudes effective immediately to resolve freight-disparity claims;
  (f) an adjustment of 1 cent per barrel increase in posted prices

immediately in the case of Iranian heavy, Saudi Arabian medium and Kuwaiti crudes;

(g) a gravity adjustment;

(h) elimination of OPEC allowances for percentage gravity and marketing.

After the Tehran agreement a similar agreement was signed in Tripoli and several other agreements were concluded by Iraq and Saudi Arabia concerning their Mediterranean crudes.

During their negotiations, however, the member countries of OPEC, were unaware of the *de facto* devaluation of the dollar and for that reason an agreement was signed on 20 January 1972 providing for an immediate increase of 8.49 per cent in posted prices to compensate for the devaluation of the US dollar. This agreement, which covered export of crude oil from both the Gulf and the eastern Mediterranean, recognized the effect of widespread currency changes unforeseen at the time of the Tehran agreement. Provisions were made for continued adjustment of posted prices according to a formula taking into account the arithmetical average of the exchange rates of currencies. However, in March 1973 OPEC called for an extraordinary conference at which international monetary problems and their implications for the oil-exporting countries were discussed. The conference resulted in another Geneva agreement, effective from June 1973, which led to a 6.1 per cent increase in posted prices.

Nevertheless OPEC was soon to change from the principle of negotiation, as a result of the stubbornness and reluctance of the oil companies and their governments to understand the economic consequences of emptying an exhaustible natural resource. On 16 October 1973, the price of Saudi 34° light oil was increased from $2.898 to $5.119 per barrel. However, the real shock came at the end of 1973 and in early 1974. World oil prices were increased to $11.15 for Kuwaiti crude. Between January 1974 and the end of 1978, posted oil prices were increased by a small percentage annually as a result of the declining value of the dollar and rising inflation. These annual increases in oil prices are shown in Table 6.1. However, despite what is called the 'oil-price explosion', the real price per barrel has been declining. In other words, the price increases of oil have not kept pace with the rate of inflation and the decline in the value of the US dollar.

As a matter of fact, the whole world in general and the industrial countries in particular should feel grateful to OPEC, because it alone

Table 6.1 *Posted prices for six major eastern hemisphere OPEC countries (US dollars per barrel): year-end prices 1960–77*

Year	Iran* Light ex Kharg Is. 34–34.9°	Iraq Basrah ex Fao 35–35.9°	Kuwait ex Mena al-Ahmadi 31–31.9°	Libya Brega ex Marsa el Brega 40–40.9°	Nigeria Arabia Light ex Bonny 34–34.9°	Saudi Arabia † ex Sidon 34–34.9°
1960	1.780	1.720	1.590			2.170
1961	1.780	1.720	1.590	2.230		2.170
1962	1.780	1.720	1.590	2.230		2.170
1963	1.780	1.720	1.590	2.230		2.170
1964	1.780	1.720	1.590	2.230		2.170
1965	1.780	1.720	1.590	2.230		2.170
1966	1.790	1.720	1.590	2.230		2.170
1967	1.790	1.720	1.590	2.230	2.170	2.170
1968	1.790	1.720	1.590	2.230	2.170	2.170
1969	1.790	1.720	1.590	2.230	2.170	2.170
1970	1.790	1.720	1.680	2.550	2.420	2.370
1971	2.274	2.259‡	2.187	3.399	3.178	3.136
1972	2.467	2.451‡	2.373	3.620	3.409	3.321
1973	5.254	4.978‡	4.822	9.061	8.404	7.034
1974	11.475	11.272‡	11.145	15.768	14.691	13.247
1975	12.495	12.400	12.151	16.060	13.070	**
1976	12.495	12.400	12.151	16.060	13.070	**
1977††	13.774	12.400‡†	12.151‡†	18.250	15.250‡†	**

*	Prior to 1966 port of export was Bandur Mashur.
†	API gravity for crude is 36–36.9° from 1950–6.
‡	Ex Khor-al-Amaya.
**	Not available.
††	June effective postings.
‡†	Unofficial estimate.

Source: For 1960–75, *Twentieth Century Petroleum Statistics 1976*, De Golyer & MacNaughton, Dallas, Texas. For 1976–7 *Petroleum Economist*, 'OPEC Oil Report', p. 49.

reminded the rest of the world about the seriousness of the coming energy crisis and its implications for the world economy and world peace. The age of great oil discoveries has probably come to an end. During the next decade, oil discoveries will not exceed 20 billion barrels a year. Consequently, the production-to-reserve ratio will decline to twenty-three years. It is during these coming twenty-three years that the world must come up with a new, alternative energy resource. Coal has great potential but with substantial drawbacks. Only nuclear energy is, at the present time, technically and economically feasible. However, its wide development is hindered by environmental factors and the problems of the proliferation of atomic weapons. It is fortunate that OPEC forced a low rate of oil consumption upon the OECD countries. Nevertheless, the OECD countries are not taking serious measures to help themselves and the rest of the world, through a rational practical conservation policy. Nor are they embarking on final national energy policies. The effect of rising crude-oil prices reduced the prevailing rate of oil consumption in the OECD countries from 7.2 per cent a year before 1973 to 2.5 per cent in 1975. The OECD countries will have to reduce their annual rate of oil consumption still further, for otherwise the industrial countries will have to compete for oil by the mid-1980s. The consequences of such a situation on the cohesion of the western world would be grave and could not be avoided unless the industrial world had a new, alternative source of energy available. Military invasion of some of the oil-producing countries in the Gulf region could not be excluded, because oil is a matter of life and death.

On the supply side, the economics of a depletable natural resource are obvious. Supplies are not influenced by the prevailing oil prices but by the expected future prices. Moreover, in the case of the oil-exporting countries, it is not only future oil revenues that are at stake but statehood and nationhood and their very survival, because many of the OPEC countries are completely dependent on one national resource: oil. Remove the oil sector and everything would collapse. Yet the rest of the world was cursing OPEC for increasing oil prices and blaming it for initiating inflation in the world. Unfortunately, the price of oil has not been increased to the expected future prices of oil, otherwise the whole world would have received a good lesson in the problems pertaining to waste control. As far as inflation is concerned, the price of world imports and exports was increasing by more than 6 per cent between 1970 and 1972, and during the twelve months before what is now called the 'oil-price explosion' world prices increased by more than 30 per cent. It is the industrial countries that should be blamed for initiating and exporting inflation, not the member countries of OPEC. The latter are only involved in managing the prices of crude oil and not restoring its real prices. The restoration of the real prices of oil will be the future task of OPEC. Probably, the future floor of oil prices will be based on, and compared to, the marginal cost of alternative sources of energy, taking into account all the elements of cost, including research and development, subsidies and other hidden costs.

As mentioned earlier the oil industry, since its inception, has never been exposed to a really competitive market. Neither governments nor oil companies were ready to subject the oil industry to competition. Oil prices were regulated by the Texas Railroad Commission in the USA as a result of US Government conservation policy in the 1930s. At that time nobody accused the USA of strangling the rest of the world. Yet when OPEC tried to follow a reasonable conservation policy the Western economists and politicians voiced protests ranging from nicely plated economic indignation to loosely expressed loud nonsense. After 1930 the oil companies, and in particular the major oil companies, were the messengers of oil prices and products worldwide. Their administration of oil prices and products was almost always in line with the wishes of their home governments. They were considered by the western governments and Japan as the main provider of the treasuries with substantial financial resources. It is only in the late 1960s and after, that OPEC started to have an administrative influence on oil prices, but never on product prices because the latter are still managed by the governments of the consuming countries.

The gradual increase in oil prices has added more income per barrel to the governments of the oil-exporting countries. The average revenue per barrel increased from $0.71 in 1960 to $3.45 on 16 October 1973. By the end of January 1977, the governments' average revenue per barrel had increased to $12.16, as shown in Table 6.2. That rate of increase could hardly defeat the rising rate of inflation. It is a pity that oil prices started to increase very late in the history of the economic development of the member countries of OPEC. For the past 30 years, most of the oil-exporting countries have been trying their best to develop but they have been hampered by lack of financial resources and effective management.

When oil prices started to increase in early 1970, the member countries were all caught by surprise and consequently no economic plans for future investment were ready to absorb the available financial resources. This situation led to economic waste on a large scale. At the same time large amounts of dollars were deposited with western banks in general and American Banks in particular, losing value as time passed. This situation is still prevalent as far as the surplus capital of oil-exporting countries such as Kuwait, Saudi Arabia, Qatar and Abu Dhabi are concerned. Had oil prices increased at higher rates in the 1930s, instead of

Table 6.2 *Producer government revenues: average per barrel*

	US dollars		US dollars
1960	0.71	1 January 1970	0.91
1961	0.70	14 November 1970	0.98
1962	0.71	15 February 1971	1.27
1963	0.75	20 January 1972	1.45
1964	0.75	1 June 1973	1.82
1965	0.76	16 October 1973	3.45
1966	0.77	1 January 1974	9.31
1067	0.80	1 July 1974	9.41
1968	0.83	1 October 1974	9.74
1969	0.84	1 November 1974	10.14
		1 October 1975	11.00
		1 January 1977	11.57[*]
			12.16[*]

[*] Two-tier pricing in effect January–June 1977.

Source: 1960-9 Citibank, New York, 'Average Eastern Hemisphere Production Payments to Governments'; 1970-7 Shell International Petroleum Company, based on Arabian Light 34°; *Petroleum Economist*: 'OPEC Oil Report', p. 5.

declining, a lot of economic waste could have been avoided and most of the oil-exporting countries could have built their basic infrastructure and by now they should have been at a more advanced stage of social and economic development. However, political and economic factors on the part of the industrial consuming nations and oil companies prevented that happening. The OECD countries were eager to keep the price of oil as cheap as possible, and continue to be so. Yet, in spite of the so-called 'oil-price explosion' the governments of the European countries and Japan are deriving more income per barrel from oil than the oil-exporting countries themselves. Table 6.3 shows that in 1961 the oil-exporting governments received only 6 per cent of the final consuming value of a barrel of oil, while the European governments achieved 52 per cent of the final consuming value of a barrel of oil. The balance of 42 per cent accrued to the oil companies. By 1975, the picture had not changed much. The oil-exporting countries increased their revenue to 30 per cent of the final value of a barrel of oil while the consuming countries achieved 45 per cent and the oil companies received 25 per cent in terms of profits and other elements of cost. The increase from 6 per cent to 30 per cent over the period 1961 to 1975 was mainly related to the prices of crude oil per barrel. However, the high percentage of revenue going to the oil companies and western European

Table 6.3 *Distribution of gains per barrel of oil among oil-exporting countries, oil companies and European oil-importing countries (US dollars per barrel)*

	1961 $	%	1970 $	%	1971 $	%	1972 $	%	1973 $	%	1974 $	%	1975 $	%
Revenue of producing Government*	0.76	6	0.86	6	1.35	8	1.60	9	2.30	11	9.10	34	10.10	30
Taxes by consuming Government in Europe†	7.10	52	8.30	57	8.70	55	9.40	55	11.40	56	10.30	39	14.90	45
Company margins and various cost elements	5.70	42	5.30	37	5.90	37	6.00	35	6.80	33	7.30	27	8.20	25
Total weighted average	13.60	100	14.50	100	15.90	100	17.00	100	20.50	100	26.70	100	33.20	100

* On the basis of the marker crude.

† Calculated on weighted average of products consumption patterns.

Source: A. M. Jaidah, Pricing of Oil: the Basic Facts, OPEC Special Fund, 19XX, p. 9. (Information derived from product prices and taxes published in *Petroleum Times*.)

governments was mainly derived from import duties on crude oil and indirect taxes on oil products. Nevertheless, the consuming European governments did collect more than $7 per final consuming barrel in 1961 and more than doubled their revenue per barrel by the end of 1975. The oil-exporting countries have increased their revenue per barrel more than ten times between 1961 and 1975. The oil companies did well but under the squeeze from the oil-exporting countries on the one hand and the consuming nations on the other, their revenue per barrel did not rise at the same rate as that of the oil-exporting countries or the oil-consuming governments. Nevertheless, the oil companies have always exploited certain tight-supply situations where they have charged very high prices for the oil they have bought at lower prices from the oil-exporting countries. They have always sold large quantities of oil at high prices in the spot market. This kind of behaviour by the oil companies in general and the major oil companies in particular is irritating to the oil-consuming and oil-exporting countries alike. The latter will probably not be able to allow the oil companies to continue reaping higher profits at the expense of the oil-exporting countries, which are always blamed for higher oil prices by the oil-consuming nations. Most likely, future international oil transactions will be on government-to-government bases. When that situation prevails, a large number of oil-trading companies will find themselves out of business.

Notes

Notes to Introduction

1 Mr K. Al-Adsani, the first Secretary of the first Legislative Council in Kuwait, wrote extensively about Shaikh Sabah and his role in establishing peace and security in Kuwait. See his book (in Arabic), *Establishment of Parliamentary Rule in Kuwait*, Fahad Al-Marzouk Publishing House, 1947–78, p. 20.

Notes to Chapter 1

1 J. G. Lorimer, *Gazette of the Persian Gulf, Oman and Central Arabia*, Calcutta, Superintendent Government Printing, 1908–15, vol. 1, p. 164 and table on p. 2, 252; also *A Handbook of Arabia*, Admiralty War Staff Great Britain, p. 314.
2 Political Agency report, Kuwait, 1924, 1925, 1926.
3 B. H. Jones, *An Account of the Transactions of His Majesty's Mission to the Court of Persia in the Year 1810–1811, To Which Is Appended a Brief History of the Wahauby*, London, 1834, pp. 13–15.
4 J. Griffiths, *Travels in Europe, Asia Minor and Arabia*, London, 1805, p. 351.
5 H. R. P. Dickson, private papers, Administrative Report on Kuwait, Political Agency, 1930, 1931, 1932.

Notes to Chapter 3

1 The government defines a lower-income Kuwaiti as one whose monthly income does not exceed $550.
2 The easy-finance terms offered to Kuwaitis for houses could be compared with the high rents paid by non-Kuwaitis, who are not included in the programme. This could lead to serious social tension.

Notes to Chapter 5

1 Joseph Schumpeter, *History of Economic Analysis*, New York, Oxford University Press, 1963, p. 573.
2 David McClelland, *The Achieving Society*, New York, van Nostrand, 1961, p. 105.
3 Everett E. Hagan, *On the Theory of Social Change*, Homewood, Illinois, Dorsey Press, 1962, p. 25.
4 Sayre P. Schatz, 'The Role of Capital Accumulation in Economic Development', *Journal of Development Studies*, vol. 5, no. 1, October 1968.
5 Harry Johnson, *Economic Policies Toward Less-Developed Countries*, Washington, DC, Brookings Institution, 1967, p. 46.
6 A. Lewis, *The Theory of Economic Growth*, Homewood, Illinois, Irwin, 1955, p. 57.
7 *The Petroleum Handbook*, London, Shell Petroleum Company Ltd, 1959, p. 13.
8 *Statistical Review of the World Oil Industry*, British Petroleum, London, 1965, p. 22.
9 Peter Odell, *An Economic Geography of Oil*, London, Bell, 1963, p. 112.
10 *The First Report on Coordination Oil Refinery Expansion in the OEEC Countries*, Paris, OEEC, October 1949.
11 Ministry of the Interior, *Law of Naturalization*, Kuwait Government Press, 1966, p. 3.
12 *Ibid.*, p. 5.
13 Emile Durkheim, *The Division of Labour in Society*, New York, Free Press, 7th edition, 1969, p. 14.

Notes to Chapter 6

1 Walter Levy, 'The Past, Present and Likely Future Price Structure of the International Oil Trade', *Third World Petroleum Congress Proceedings*, Leiden, E. J. Brill, 1951, section X, p. 116.
2 A basing-point system is in essence a system in which all sellers, no matter where located, calculate delivered prices in any market by taking generally accepted f.o.b. prices at one (if it is a single basing-point system) or more (if it is dual or multiple) specified locations (basing points) or adding standardised freight charges (not actual freight payments) from the basing point to the place to which the commodity is shipped, regardless of the actual origin of the commodity. Such a pricing system is a very effective device for ensuring not only that uniform delivered prices are quoted by all sellers, but also that low-cost producers cannot use their lower costs to expand

their share of the market by reducing prices. The system is restrictive precisely because, when adhered to by all sellers, it prevents the expansion of low-cost production by price competition.

Edith Penrose, 'The Movement of Crude Oil Prices Immediately After the Second World War: An Interpretation of Economic History', in *Middle East Economic Papers*, Economic Research Institute, American University of Beirut, 1967, p. 112.

3   Edith Penrose, *The Large International Firm in Developing Countries, The International Petroleum Industry*, Cambridge, Massachusetts, MIT 1968, p. 186.

4   Paul He. Frankel, *Oil: The Facts of Life*, London, Weidenfeld & Nicolson, 1962, p. 12.

Index